CHOOSING TO LOVE
THE WORLD

THOMAS MERTON

CHOOSING TO LOVE THE WORLD

ON CONTEMPLATION

Edited by Jonathan Montaldo of
The Merton Institute for Contemplative Living

SOUNDS TRUE
awakening wisdom

Sounds True, Inc.
Boulder, CO 80306

© 2008 Thomas Merton
Edited by Jonathan Montaldo
SOUNDS TRUE is a trademark of Sounds True, Inc.
All rights reserved. Published 2008.

Printed in Canada

Book design by Jennifer Miles

10 9 8 7 6 5 4 3 2 1

ISBN 978-1-59179-804-0

Library of Congress Cataloging-in-Publication Data

Merton, Thomas, 1915-1968.
  Choosing to love the world : on contemplation / the Merton Institute for
Contemplative Living ; selected and edited by Jonathan Montaldo.
      p. cm.
  Includes bibliographical references.
  ISBN 978-1-59179-804-0 (hardcover)
  1. Spirituality—Catholic Church. 2. Meditations. 3. Contemplation. I.
Montaldo, Jonathan. II. Merton Institute for Contemplative Living. III.
Title.

BX2350.65.M46 2008
242—dc22

                              2007048308

⊕ This book is printed on recycled paper containing 100% post-consumer waste
and processed without chlorine.

CHOOSING TO LOVE THE WORLD

CONTENTS

INTRODUCTION

*If the deepest ground of my being is love, then
in that very love and nowhere else will I find
myself, the world, and my brother and sister
in Christ. It is not a question of either-or but
of all-in-one. It is not a matter of exclusivity
and "purity" but of wholeness, wholeheartedness, unity, and of Meister Eckhart's gleichheit
(equality) which finds the same ground of love
in everything.*

THOMAS MERTON, *Contemplation in a World of Action*

The American writer Thomas Merton (1915–1968), a monk of The Abbey of Gethsemani in Nelson County, Kentucky, for twenty-seven years, possessed an inclusive, un-walled spirit. Sorrowed by the wars of his time, he affiliated himself with his generation as it rode the waves of the twentieth century's harshest flow of events. Whereas an older school of monastic observance warned monks to abandon "the world" as decisively as one flees a sinking ship, Merton's monastic project was a blend of world-engaging actions: he prayed, wrote books, and, as a mature monk, publicly protested any perspective that threatened the unity of all beings that was at the heart of what he believed "real" in human experience. Merton contributed to and loved what he conceived to be the world's "real" history, the flow of events coproduced by the thought and action of each singular, potentially lovely, member of the one body that is our humankind.

Merton wrote in a variety of genres: poetry, meditative prose, the scholarly article, political polemic, dramatic pieces, song cycles, autobiography, and the personal letter and journal. He was among the first Roman Catholic American writers with a popular audience to share his enthusiasm for contemplative traditions other than his own. His reading in Buddhist, Islamist, Hindu, Jewish, Taoist, and Confucian traditions bore fruit in his personal contacts with an international spectrum of contemplatives and scholars of religion. Merton's influence continues to affect those committed to contemplative living and interfaith dialogue in the twenty-first century.

Educated in France and England, receiving his undergraduate and graduate degrees from Columbia University in New York City, Merton challenged the distorted perspectives of a monocultural approach to relationships. His contemplative life supported his life's project to free himself and his neighbors from what he called the "obligatory answers" prescribed and enforced by their educations, their racial and national heritages, their religious tribes, and any of their institutions that thrived by dividing human beings into family and strangers.

In 1941, at the age of twenty-seven, Merton entered a rigorous discipline of personal transformation in a Trappist monastery, where strict rules programmed every aspect of its members' daily lives. And yet this institutionalized life of prayer provided him with disciplines necessary for the inner work to transcend its narrow boundaries and free his religious imagination to view God as a limitless horizon. Merton taught his readers that true religion should always make them personally and communally free. In *Conjectures of a Guilty Bystander,* one of his best books, as relevant today as ever, he wrote that true religion always nurtures "freedom from domination, freedom to live one's own spiritual life, freedom to seek the highest truth, unabashed by any human pressure or any collective demand, the ability to say one's own 'yes' and one's own 'no' and not merely to echo the 'yes' and the 'no' of state, party, corporation, army or system. This is inseparable from authentic religion. It is one of the deepest and most fundamental needs of the human person, perhaps the deepest and most crucial need of the human person as such."

Merton never held "the world" at arm's length. The world for him was more than "a physical space traversed by jet planes and full of people running in all directions," offering a monk only one of two choices: to fight or flee. His world was no objective "thing" directed by impersonal forces that rendered humankind without liberty to act the way we act and live for what we live. For Merton, the world was always being reconfigured through "a complex of responsibilities and options made out of the love, the hates, the fears, the joys, the hopes, the greed, the cruelty, the kindness, the faith, the trust, the suspicion of all."

Merton embraced monastic life as a protest against his own false self. He vowed himself to inner struggle against the ego-centered individualism embedded in his psyche. By becoming a monk, he hoped to marginalize himself from the mental geography of "the impatient ones who conceived reality in terms of money, power, publicity, machines, business, political advantage, military strategy—who seek the triumphant affirmation of their own will, their own power considered as the end for which they exist." Merton rarely minced words as he pierced through the patina of American innocence and idealism to confront the metallic hardness of its national greed, pride, and misdirected lust to be first in everything. But if his monastic life rendered him a "marginal person" to the dominant materialistic paradigm of American society, he never renounced his citizenship or his responsibility to put his whole self to work in shifting America's priorities: "Man has a responsibility to his own time, not as if he could seem to stand outside it and donate various spiritual and material benefits to it from a position of compassionate distance. Man has a responsibility to find himself where he is, in his own proper time and place, in the history to which he belongs and to which he must inevitably contribute either his response or his evasions, either truth and act, or mere slogan and gesture."

The biting criticisms of contemporary Western culture gathered in this book are balanced by those passages that reveal a poet of his inner experiences who was aware of his own fragile grasp on truth. Thus, in judging personal matters through which all human beings suffer, he was never fundamentalist. Admitting the complexity and the paradoxes attending his own life, he renounced an intellectual's obsession to nail every human ethical question to the floor. He was conscious of his need for lifelong learning to render himself better able to decipher the deeper subtexts of his own life's and his world's flow of events. His writing exhibits his constant attention to a diverse, mixed chorus of other voices. He exuded religious enthusiasm for tracking God's presence in and for the world, a presence which he apprehended as profoundly personal. Merton's theology was lived: God surged in all our bloodstreams, "within the stream of reality of life itself."

In all his writing, Merton characterizes the contemplative life as a life of relationships informed by love in search of freedom. We are the primary actors in the formation of our own identities. We create networks of nurturing interrelationships with our fellow human beings. We affect and are affected by the matrix of nature's evolution within which we move and have our being. Through this trinity of relationships, we experience communion with the Source that underwrites our being in time, the *Logos* that energizes our becoming "one with everything in that hidden ground of love for which there can be no explanations." Contemplation is a deepening awareness of and attention to all our relationships; it is the deciphering in real time of the essential unity of all beings; it is an active consciousness that knows with certitude that the world is ours and that we are God's. "It {the world} dictates no terms to man. We and our world interpenetrate. If anything, the world exists for us, and we exist for ourselves. It is only in assuming full responsibility for our world, for our lives and for ourselves, that we can be said to live really for God."

Merton taught that contemplation is for everyone and that the context for seeking God's presence is always our everyday lives. In unpublished notes for a conference he had prepared for his monastic novices on "prayer," Merton urged them to meditate by entering "the school of their lives," to meditate upon the events of their lives as a "school of wisdom" in which they were being taught to become their truest selves. He reminded his students that contemplation is "a response to a call: a call from Him Who has no voice, and yet Who speaks in everything that is, and Who, most of all, speaks in the depths of our own being: for we ourselves are words of His." Thus, contemplation was attentiveness to the "words" God was always speaking through their most personal experiences. To hear God's voice, they needed to ruminate on the daily direction of their hearts' desires. This way of praying, however, would never be automatic. They would have to make conscious decisions to instigate their contemplative lives: "Either you look at the universe as a very poor creation out of which no one can make anything, or you look at your own life and your own part in the universe as infinitely rich, full of inexhaustible interest, opening out into the infinite further responsibilities for study and contemplation and interest and praise. Beyond all and in all is God."

May these reflections on contemplation encourage our own decisions to decipher the inner ground of Love that supports us through our lives' flow of events. In our time sorrowed by new wars, may we affiliate with all who are transforming the "world" by exercising their inner options for peace in all that they are doing. May these reflections mentor confidence in our inexhaustibly rich vocation to be fully alive as joy-filled, compassionate and un-walled-up human beings. A month before his death in Bangkok, Thailand, by accidental electrocution on December 10, 1968, Thomas Merton gave his contemplative life's project an unintended final summary in a talk he gave in Calcutta, India:

> I stand among you as one who offers a small message of hope, that first, there are always people who dare to seek on the margin of society, who are not dependent on social acceptance, not dependent on social routine, and prefer a kind of free-floating existence under a state of risk. And among these people, if they are faithful to their own calling, to their own vocation, and to their own message from God,

communication on the deepest level is possible. And the deepest level of communication is not communication, but communion. It is wordless. It is beyond words, and it is beyond speech, and it is beyond concept. Not that we discover a new unity. We discover an older unity. My dear brothers and sisters, we are already one. But we imagine that we are not. So what we have to recover is our original unity. What we have to be is what we are.

JONATHAN MONTALDO
The Merton Institute for Contemplative Living
Louisville, Kentucky

1 | THE INNER GROUND OF LOVE

The solution of the problem of life is life itself.

Life is not attained by reason and analysis

but first of all by living.

THOUGHTS IN SOLITUDE

We prescribe for one another remedies that will bring us peace of mind, and we are still devoured by anxiety. We evolve plans for disarmament and for the peace of nations, and our plans only change the manner and method of aggression. The rich have everything they want except happiness, and the poor are sacrificed to the unhappiness of the rich. Dictatorships use their secret police to crush millions under an intolerable burden of lies, injustice and tyranny, and those who still live in democracies have forgotten how to make good use of their liberty. For liberty is a thing of the spirit, and we are no longer able to live for anything but our bodies. How can we find peace, true peace, if we forget that we are not machines for making and spending money, but spiritual beings, sons and daughters of the most high God?

That I should have been born in 1915, that I should be the contemporary of Auschwitz, Hiroshima, Viet Nam and the Watts riots, are things about which I was not first consulted. Yet they are also events in which, whether I like it or not, I am deeply and personally involved. The "world" is not just a physical space traversed by jet planes and full of people running in all directions. It is a complex of responsibilities and options made out of the love, the hates, the fears, the joys, the hopes, the greed, the cruelty, the kindness, the faith, the trust, the suspicion of all. In the last analysis, if there is war because nobody trusts anybody, this is in part because I myself am defensive, suspicious, untrusting, and intent on making other people conform themselves to my particular brand of death wish.

If I had no choice about the age in which I was to live, I nevertheless have a choice about the attitude I take and about the way and the extent of my participation in its living ongoing events. To choose the world is not then merely a pious admission that the world is acceptable because it comes from the hand of God. It is first of all an acceptance of a task and a vocation in the world, in history and in time. In my time, which is the present. To choose the world is to choose to do the work I am capable of doing, in collaboration with my brother and sister, to make the world better, more free, more just, more livable, more human. And it has now become transparently obvious that mere automatic "rejection of the world" and "contempt for the world" is in fact not a choice but an evasion of choice. The person who pretends that he can turn his back on Auschwitz or Viet Nam and act as if they were not there, is simply bluffing.

I have a profound mistrust of all obligatory answers. The great problem of our time is not to formulate clear answers to neat theoretical questions but to tackle the self-destructive alienation of man in a society dedicated in theory to human values and in practice to the pursuit of power for its own sake. All the new and fresh answers in the world, all the bright official confidence in the collectivity of the secular city, will do nothing to change the reality of this alienation. The Marxist worldview is the really coherent and systematic one that has so far come forward to replace the old medieval Christian and classical synthesis. It has in fact got itself accepted, for better or for worse, by more than half the human race. And yet, while claiming to offer man hope of deliverance from alienation, it has demanded a more unquestioning, a more irrational and a more submissive obedience than ever to its obligatory answers, even when these are *manifestly self-contradictory and destructive of the very values they claim to defend.*

When "the world" is hypostatized [regarded as a distinct reality] (and it inevitably is), it becomes another of those dangerous and destructive fictions with which we are trying vainly to grapple. And for anyone who has seriously entered into the medieval Christian, or the Hindu, or the Buddhist conceptions of *contemptus mundi* [hatred for the world], Mara and the "emptiness of the world," it will be evident that this means not the rejection of a reality, but the unmasking of an illusion. The world as pure object is something that is not there. It is not a reality outside us for which we exist. It is not a firm and absolute objective structure which has to be accepted on its own inexorable terms. The world has in fact no terms of its own. It dictates no terms to man. We and our world interpenetrate. If anything, the world exists for us, and we exist for ourselves. It is only in assuming full responsibility for our world, for our lives and for ourselves that we can be said to live really for God.

The aggressive and dominative view of reality places, at the center, the individual with its bodily form, its feelings and emotions, its appetites and needs, its loves and hates, its actions and reactions. All these are seen as forming together a basic and indubitable reality to which everything else must be referred, so that all other things are also estimated in their individuality, their actions and reactions, and all the ways in which they impinge upon the interests of the individual self. The world is then seen as a multiplicity of conflicting and limited beings, all enclosed in the limits of their own individuality, all therefore complete in a permanent and vulnerable incompleteness, all seeking to find a certain completeness by asserting themselves at the expense of others, dominating and using others. The world becomes, then, an immense conflict in which the only peace is that which is accorded to the victory of the strong, and in order to taste the joy of this peace, the weak must submit to the strong and join them in their adventures so that they may share in their power.

Only when we see ourselves in our true human context, as members of a race which is intended to be one organism and "one body," will we begin to understand the positive importance not only of the successes but of the failures and accidents in our lives. My successes are not my own. The way to them was prepared by others. The fruit of my labors is not my own: for I am preparing the way for the achievements of another. Nor are my failures my own. They may spring from the failure of another, but they are also compensated for by another's achievement. Therefore the meaning of my life is not to be looked for merely in the sum total of my achievements. It is seen only in the complete integration of my achievements and failures with the achievements and failures of my own generation, and society, and time. It is seen, above all, in my own integration in Christ.

The whole human reality, which of course transcends us as individuals and as a collectivity, nevertheless interpenetrates the world of nature (which is obviously "real") and the world of history (also "real" insofar as it is made up of the total effect of all our decisions and actions). But this reality, though "external" and "objective," is not something entirely independent of us, which dominates us inexorably from without through the medium of certain fixed laws which science alone can discover and use. It is an extension and a projection of ourselves and of our lives, and, if we attend to it respectfully, while attending also to our own freedom and our own integrity, we can learn to obey its ways and coordinate our lives with its mysterious movements.

The way to find the real "world" is not merely to measure and observe what is outside us, but to discover our own inner ground. For that is where the world is, first of all: in my deepest self. But there I find the world to be quite different from the "obligatory answers." This "ground," this "world" where I am mysteriously present at once to my own self and to the freedoms of all other men, is not a visible, objective and determined structure with fixed laws and demands. It is a living and self-creating mystery of which I am myself a part, to which I am myself my own unique door. When I find the world in my own ground, it is impossible for me to be alienated by it. It is precisely the obligatory answers which insist on showing the world as totally other than me and my neighbors, which alienate me from myself and from my neighbors. Hence I see no reason for our compulsion to manufacture ever newer and shinier sets of obligatory answers.

The true solutions are not those which we force upon life in accordance with our theories, but those which life itself provides for those who dispose themselves to receive the truth. Consequently our task is to dissociate ourselves from all who have theories which promise clear-cut and infallible solutions, and to mistrust all such theories, not in a spirit of negativism and defeat, but rather trusting life itself, and nature, and if you will permit me, God above all. For since man has decided to occupy the place of God he has shown himself to be by far the blindest, and cruelest, and pettiest, and most ridiculous of all the false gods.

There remains a profound wisdom in the traditional Christian approach to the world as an object of choice. But we have to admit that the habitual and mechanical compulsions of a certain limited type of Christian thought have falsified the true value-perspective in which the world can be discovered and chosen as it is. To treat the world merely as an agglomeration of material goods and objects outside ourselves, and to reject these goods and objects in order to seek others which are "interior" and "spiritual" is in fact to miss the whole point of the challenging confrontation of the world and Christ. Do we really choose between the world and Christ as between two conflicting realities absolutely opposed? Or do we choose Christ by choosing the world as it really is in Him, that is to say created and redeemed by Him, and encountered in the ground of our own personal freedom and of our love?

Do we really renounce ourselves and the world in order to find Christ, or do we renounce our alienated and false selves in order to choose our own deepest truth in choosing both the world and Christ at the same time? If the deepest ground of my being is love, then in that very love and nowhere else will I find myself, the world, and my brother and my sister in Christ. It is not a question of either-or but of all-in-one. It is not a matter of exclusivity and "purity" but of wholeness, wholeheartedness, unity, and of Meister Eckhart's *gleichheit* (equality) which finds the same ground of love in everything.

I think . . . that this kind of view of reality is essentially very close to the Christian monastic view of reality. It is the view that, if you once penetrate by detachment and purity of heart to the inner secret ground of your ordinary experience, you attain to a liberty that nobody can touch, that nobody can affect, that no political change of circumstances can do anything to. I admit this is a bit idealistic. I have not attempted to see how this works in a concentration camp, and I hope I will not have the opportunity. But I am just saying that somewhere behind our [Christian] monasticism, and behind Buddhist monasticism, is the belief that this kind of freedom and transcendence is somehow attainable.

The begging bowl of the Buddha represents . . . the ultimate theological root of the belief not just in the right to be, but in openness to the gifts of all beings as an expression of the interdependence of all beings. This is the most central concept of Buddhism—or at least in Mahayana Buddhism.

The whole idea of compassion, which is central to Mahayana Buddhism, is based on a keen awareness of the interdependence of all these living beings, which are all part of one another and all involved in one another. Thus when the monk begs from the layman and receives a gift from the layman, it is not as a selfish person getting something from somebody else. He is simply opening himself to this interdependence, this mutual interdependence, in which they all recognize that they all are immersed in illusion together, but that the illusion is also an empirical reality that has to be fully accepted, and that in this illusion, which is nevertheless empirically real, *nirvana* is present and it is all there, if you but see it.

The world cannot be a problem to anyone who sees that ultimately Christ, the world, his sister, his brother, and his own inmost ground are made one and the same in grace and redemptive love. If all the current talk about the world helps people to discover this, then it is fine. But if it produces nothing but a whole new divisive gamut of obligatory positions and "contemporary answers," we might as well forget it. The world itself is no problem, but we are a problem to ourselves because we are alienated from ourselves, and this alienation is due precisely to an inveterate habit of division by which we break reality into pieces and then wonder why, after we have manipulated the pieces until they fall apart, we find ourselves out of touch with life, with reality, with the world, and most of all with ourselves.

As Dietrich Bonheoffer once observed, God is not simply a stopgap for the holes in our knowledge of the world, nor is He merely the source of ultimate answers to personal and human problems. In other words, God is not simply the one Whom we reach when we are extended to our limits. He is, on the contrary, the ground and center of our existence, and though we may conceive ourselves as "going to" Him and reaching out to Him beyond the sphere of our everyday existence, we nevertheless start from Him and remain in Him as the very ground of our existence and reality.

He is not merely "out there" in a vague beyond. He is not merely hidden in the shadows of what is unknown and pushed further and further away in proportion as we come to know more and more. He is the very ground of what we know and our knowledge itself is His manifestation: not that He is the cause of all that is real, but that reality itself is His epiphany.

The words of Bonheoffer are profoundly biblical in their radical dismissal of "unworldly" faith that centers too exclusively on personal crisis and on the quest for an inner refuge from worldly conflict. It was not from the Bible that we learned to escape "into eternity," nor did the Bible teach us to seek peace in inwardness and defensive recollection. These are elements of another cultural and spiritual heritage. As Bonheoffer says:

> We should find God in what we know, not in what we don't; not in outstanding problems but in those we have already solved . . . .We must not wait until we are at the end of our tether: he must be found at the center of life and not only in death; in health and vigor, and not only in suffering; in activity, and not only in sin. (*Prison Letters*, p. 191)

The Bible is a "worldly" book in the sense that it sees God at the very center of man's life, his work, his relations with his fellow man, his play and his joy. On the contrary, it is characteristic of the idols that they are objectified and set up on the periphery of life. It is the idols who dominate specific areas of life from outside it, because they are in fact projections of man's fragmented desires and aspirations. It is the idols that man goes out to meet when he reaches his own limit, and they are called in to supplement his strength and his ingenuity when these run out. God is never shown by the Bible merely as a *supplement* of man's power and intelligence, but as its very ground and reality.

We live on the brink of disaster because we do not know how to let life alone. We do not respect the living and fruitful contradictions and paradoxes of which true life is full. We destroy them, or try to destroy them, with our obsessive and absurd systematizations. Whether we do this in the name of matter or in the name of spirit makes little difference in the end. There are atheists who fight God and atheists who claim to believe in Him: what they both have in common is the hatred of life, the fear of the unpredictable, the dread of grace, and the refusal of every spiritual gift.

What is wanted now is not simply the Christian who takes an inner complacency in the words and example of Christ, but who seeks to follow Christ perfectly, not only in his own personal life, not only in prayer and penance, but also in his political commitments and in all social responsibilities.

We have certainly no need for a pseudo-contemplative spirituality that claims to ignore the world and its problems entirely, and devotes itself supposedly to the things of God, without concern for human society. All true Christian spirituality, even that of the Christian contemplative, is and must always be deeply concerned with man, since "God became man in order that man might become God" (St. Irenaeus). The Christian spirit is one of compassion, of responsibility and of commitment. It cannot be indifferent to suffering, to injustice, error, and untruth.

Life consists in learning to live on one's own, spontaneous, freewheeling: to do this one must recognize what is one's own—be familiar and at home with oneself. This means basically learning who one is, and learning what one has to offer the contemporary world, and then learning how to make that offering valid.

The purpose of education is to show persons how to define themselves authentically and spontaneously in relation to their world—not to impose a prefabricated definition of the world, still less an arbitrary definition of individuals themselves. The world is made up of the people who are fully alive in it and can enter into a living and fruitful relationship with each other in it. The world is therefore more real in proportion as the people in it are able to be more fully and more humanly alive: that is to say, better able to make a lucid and conscious use of their freedom. Basically, this freedom must consist first of all in the capacity to choose their own lives, to find themselves on the deepest possible level.

The function of a university is, then, first of all to help students discover themselves: to recognize themselves, and to identify who it is that chooses.

This description will be recognized at once as unconventional and, in fact, monastic. To put it in even more outrageous terms, the function of the university is to help men and women save their souls and, in so doing, to save their society: from what? From the hell of meaninglessness, of obsession, of complex artifice, of systematic lying, of criminal evasions and neglects, of self-destructive futilities.

It will be evident from my context that the business of saving one's soul means more than taking an imaginary object, "a soul," and entrusting it to some institutional bank for deposit until it is recovered with interest in heaven.

Speaking as a Christian existentialist, I mean by "soul" not simply the Aristotelian essential form but the mature personal identity, the creative fruit of an authentic and lucid search, the "self" that is found after other partial and exterior selves have been discarded as masks.

I admit that all through the Middle Ages men were actively curious about the exact location of the earthly paradise. This curiosity was not absent from the mind of Columbus. The Pilgrim Fathers purified it a little, spiritualized it a little, but New England to them was a kind of paradise: and to make sure of a paradisic institution they created, of all things, Harvard. But the monks of the Middle Ages, and the clerks too, believed that the inner paradise was the ultimate ground of freedom in man's heart. To find it one had to travel, as Augustine had said, not with steps, but with yearnings. The journey was from man's "fallen" condition, in which he was not free to be true to himself, to that original freedom in which, made in the image and likeness of God, he was no longer able to be untrue to himself. Hence, he recovered that nakedness of Adam which needed no fig leaves of law, of explanation, of justification, and no social garments of skins (Gregory of Nyssa). Paradise is simply the person, the self, but the radical self in its uninhibited freedom. The self no longer clothed with an ego.

The graduate level of learning is when one learns to sit still and be what one has become, which is what one does not know and does not need to know. . . . One no longer seeks something else. One no longer seeks to be told by another who one is. One no longer demands assurance. But there is the whole infinite depth of *what is* remaining to be revealed. And it is not revealed to those who seek it from others.

Education in this sense means more than learning; and for such education, one is awarded no degree. One graduates by rising from the dead. Learning to be oneself means, therefore, learning to die in order to live. It means discovering in the ground of one's being a "self" which is ultimate and indestructible, which not only survives the destruction of all other more superficial selves but finds its identity affirmed and clarified by their destruction.

The inmost self is naked.

What is serious to men is often trivial in the sight of God. What in God might appear to us as "play" is perhaps what He Himself takes most seriously. At any rate the Lord plays and diverts Himself in the garden of His creation, and if we could let go of our own obsession with what we think is the meaning of it all, we might be able to hear His call and follow Him in His mysterious, cosmic dance. We do not have to go very far to catch echoes of that game, and of that dancing. When we are alone on a starlit night; when by chance we see the migrating birds in autumn descending on a grove of junipers to rest and eat; when we see children in a moment when they are really children; when we know love in our own hearts; or when, like the Japanese poet Basho, we hear an old frog land in a quiet pond with a solitary splash—at such times the awakening, the turning inside out of all values, the "newness," the emptiness, and the purity of vision that make themselves evident, provide a glimpse of the cosmic dance.

The world and time are the dance of the Lord in emptiness. The silence of the spheres is the music of a wedding feast. The more we persist in misunderstanding the phenomena of life, the more we analyze them out into strange finalities and complex purposes of our own, the more we involve ourselves in sadness, absurdity and despair. But it does not matter much, because no despair of ours can alter the reality of things, or stain the joy of the cosmic dance which is always there. Indeed, we are in the midst of it, and it is in the midst of us, for it beats in our very blood, whether we want it to or not.

Yet the fact remains that we are invited to forget ourselves on purpose, cast our awful solemnity to the winds and join in the general dance.

2 | LIVING IN WISDOM

What can we gain by sailing to the moon

if we cannot cross the abyss

that separates us from ourselves?

THE WISDOM OF THE DESERT

One thing I know—that it is my destiny to be a contemplative, a Christian, and an American. I can satisfy my vocation with nothing that is partial or provincial. I cannot be a "North American" who knows only the rivers, the plains, the mountains, and the cities of the north, the north where there are few Indians, where the land was colonized and cultivated by the Puritans . . . . This north is grand, powerful, rich, intelligent; it has a warmth all its own, a surprising humility, a charity, an inner purity that the stranger does not know. But it is incomplete. It is neither the better nor the richer part of the hemisphere . . . It lacks the roots of the old America, the America of Mexico and the Andes, where silent and contemplative Asians came millenniums ago to construct their hieratic [highly stylized and priestly] cities. It lacks the intense fervor and fecundity of Brazil, which is also African, which smiles with the grin of the Congo and laughs with the childlike innocence of Portugal. The northern half of this New World lacks the force, the refinement, the prodigality of Argentina with all the lyricism of its tormented and generous heart.

I cannot be a partial American and I cannot be, which is even sadder, a partial Catholic. For me Catholicism is not confined to one culture, one nation, one age, one race. My faith is not a mixture of the Irish Catholicism of the United States and the splendid and vital Catholicism, reborn during the past war, of my native France. Though I admire the cathedrals and the past of Catholicism in Latin America, my Catholicism goes beyond the Spanish tradition. I cannot believe that Catholicism is tied to the destiny of any group which confusedly expresses the economic illusions of a social class. My Catholicism is not the religion of the bourgeoisie nor will it ever be. My Catholicism is all the world and all ages. It dates from the beginning of the world.

Contemplation is life itself, fully awake, fully active, fully aware that it is alive. It is spiritual wonder. It is spontaneous awe at the sacredness of life, of being. It is gratitude for life, for awareness, and for being. It is a vivid realization of the fact that life and being in us proceed from an invisible, transcendent, and infinitely abundant Source. Contemplation is, above all, awareness of the reality of that Source. It *knows* the Source, obscurely, inexplicably, but with a certitude that goes beyond reason and beyond simple faith . . . It is a more profound depth of faith, a knowledge too deep to be grasped in images, in words, or even in clear concepts.

Poetry, music and art have something in common with the contemplative experience. But contemplation is beyond aesthetic intuition, beyond art, beyond poetry. Indeed, it is also beyond philosophy, beyond speculative theology. It resumes, transcends and fulfills them all, and yet at the same time it seems, in a certain way, to supersede and to deny them all. Contemplation is always beyond our own knowledge, beyond our own light, beyond systems, beyond explanations, beyond discourse, beyond dialogue, beyond our own self. To enter into the realm of contemplation one must in a certain sense die: but this death is in fact the entrance to a higher life. It is a death for the sake of life, which leaves behind all that we can know or treasure as life, as thought, as experience, as joy, as being.

When I speak of the contemplative life, I do not mean the institutional cloistered life, the organized life of prayer . . . . I am talking about a special dimension of inner discipline and experience, a certain integrity and fullness of personal development, which are not compatible with a purely external, alienated, busy-busy existence. This does not mean that these special dimensions are incompatible with action, with creative work, with dedicated love. On the contrary, these all go together. A certain depth of disciplined experience is a necessary ground for fruitful action. Without a more profound human understanding derived from exploration of the inner ground of human existence, love will tend to be superficial and deceptive. Traditionally, the ideas of prayer, meditation and contemplation have been associated with this deepening of one's personal life and this expansion of the capacity to understand and serve others.

He who attempts to act and do things for others or for the world without deepening his own self-understanding, freedom, integrity and capacity to love, will not have anything to give others. He will communicate to them nothing but the contagion of his own obsessions, his aggressiveness, his ego-centered ambitions, his delusions about ends and means, his doctrinaire prejudices and ideas. There is nothing more tragic in the modern world than the misuse of power and action to which we are driven by our own Faustian misunderstandings and misapprehensions. We have more power at our disposal today than we have ever had, and yet we are more alienated and estranged from the inner ground of meaning and of love than we have ever been. The result of this is evident. We are living through the greatest crisis in the history of man; and this crisis is centered precisely in the country that has made a fetish out of action and has lost (or perhaps never had) the sense of contemplation. Far from being irrelevant, prayer, meditation and contemplation are of utmost importance in America today.

The way of wisdom is not an evasion. Simply to evade modern life would be a futile attempt to abdicate from its responsibilities while clinging to its advantages. The way of contemplation is a way of higher and more permanent responsibilities and a renunciation of advantages—and illusions. The contemplative way requires first of all and above all the renunciation of this obsession with the triumph of the individual or collective will to power. For this aggressive and self-assertive drive to possess and to exert power implies a totally different view of reality than that which is seen when one travels the contemplative way.

The basic reality is neither the individual, empirical self nor an abstract and ideal entity which can exist only in reason. The basic reality is being itself, which is one in all concrete existents, which shares itself among them and manifests itself through them. The goal of the contemplative is, on its lowest level, the recognition of this splendor of being and unity—a splendor in which the contemplative is one with all that is. But on a higher level still, it is the transcendent ground and source of being, the not-being and the emptiness that is so called because it is absolutely beyond definitions and limitation. This ground and source is not simply an inert and passive emptiness, but for the Christian it is pure act, pure freedom, pure light. The emptiness which is "pure being" is the light of God which, as St. John's Gospel says, "gives light to every man who comes into the world" [John 1:9].

The Christian is then not simply a man of good will, who commits himself to a certain set of beliefs, who has a definite dogmatic conception of the universe, of man, and of man's reason for existing. He is not simply one who follows a moral code of brotherhood and benevolence with strong emphasis on certain rewards and punishments dealt out to the individual. Underlying Christianity is not simply a set of doctrines about God considered as dwelling remotely in heaven, and man struggling on earth, trying to appease a distant God by means of virtuous acts. On the contrary Christians themselves too often fail to realize that the infinite God is dwelling within them, so that He is in them and they are in Him. They remain unaware of the presence of the infinite source of being right in the midst of the world and of men. True Christian wisdom is therefore oriented to the experience of divine Light which is present in the world, the Light in whom all things are, and which is nevertheless unknown to the world because no mind can see or grasp its infinity.

ontemplative wisdom is then not simply an aesthetic extrapolation of certain intellectual or dogmatic principles, but a living contact with the Infinite Source of all being, a contact not only of minds and hearts, not only of "I and Thou," but a transcendent union of consciousness in which man and God become, according to the expression of St. Paul, "one spirit."

Though this contemplative union is an extreme intensification of conscious awareness, a kind of total awareness, it is not properly contained or signified in any particular vision, but rather in non-vision which attains the totality of meaning beyond all limiting conceptions, by the surrender of love. God Himself is not only pure being but also pure love, and to know Him is to become one with Him in love. In this dimension of Christian experience, the cross of Christ means more than the juridical redemption of man from the guilt of evil-doing. It means the passage from death to life and from nothingness to fullness, or to fullness in nothingness.

The contemplative way of ancient Christian monastic tradition is not simply a way of emptiness and transcendence in union with the crucified Christ. The cross signifies that the sacrificial death, which is indeed the destruction of the empirical bodily existence and end of all lust for earthly power and all indulgence of passion, is in fact the liberation of those who have renounced this exterior self in order to dedicate their lives to love and to truth. Christ is not simply an object of love and contemplation whom the Christian considers with devout attention. He is also "the way, the truth and the life" so that for the Christian to be "on the way" is to be "in Christ" and to seek truth is to walk in the light of Christ. "For me to live," says St. Paul, "is Christ. I live, now not I, but Christ lives in me" [Galations 2:20].

The source of wisdom, from which all men desire to drink (for all men desire happiness, and wisdom is man's happiness), cannot be discovered by the rod of the diviner. Who shall tell a man the way to this hidden fountain, springing up from beyond the inmost essence of things? . . .

And yet, paradoxically, this wisdom cries out in the streets, and waits for men, calling to them and beckoning in the gates of the city and in the marketplace. But men pass by without finding wisdom. For in order to find her they must hide her commandments in their heart (Proverbs 2:1) by "keeping" them. For that is what it means to "keep" a commandment. It means not only to remember it but to make it part of one's own being by doing what it says.

We have an instinctive need for harmony and peace, for tranquility, order and meaning. None of these seem to be the most salient characteristics of modern society. . . . We must face the fact that the mere thought of contemplation is one which deeply troubles the person who takes it seriously. It is so contrary to the modern way of life, so apparently alien, so seemingly impossible, that the modern man who even considers it finds, at first, that his whole being rebels against it. If the ideal of inner peace remains attractive, the demands of the way to peace seem to be so exacting and extreme that they can no longer be met. We would like to be quiet, but our restlessness will not allow it. Hence we believe that for us there can be no peace except in a life filled with movement and activity, with speech, news, communication, recreation, distraction. We seek the meaning of our life in activity for its own sake, activity without objective, efficacy without fruit, scientism, the cult of unlimited power, the service of the machine as an end in itself.

The life of frantic activity is invested with the noblest of qualities, as if it were the whole end and happiness of man: or rather, as if the life of man had no inherent meaning whatever and that it had to be given a meaning from some external source, from a society engaged in a gigantic communal effort to raise man above himself. Man is indeed called to transcend himself. But do his own efforts suffice for this?

The reason for this inner confusion and conflict is that our technological society has no longer any place in it for wisdom that seeks truth for its own sake, that seeks the fullness of being, that seeks to rest in an intuition of the very ground of all being. Without wisdom, the apparent opposition of action and contemplation, of work and rest, of involvement and detachment, can never be resolved.

Ancient and traditional societies, whether of Asia or of the West, always specifically recognized "the way" of the wise, the way of spiritual discipline in which there was at once wisdom and method, and by which, whether in art, in philosophy, in religion, or in the monastic life, some would attain to the inner meaning of being, they would *experience* this meaning for all, they would so to speak bring together in themselves the division or complications that confused the life of their fellows. By healing the divisions in themselves they would help heal the divisions of the world. They would realize in themselves the unity which is at the same time the highest action and the purest rest, true knowledge and self-less love, a knowledge beyond knowledge in emptiness and unknowing; a willing beyond will in apparent non-activity. They would attain to the highest striving in the absence of striving and of contention.

The contemplative life must provide an area, a space of liberty, of silence, in which possibilities are allowed to surface and new choices—beyond routine choice—become manifest. It should create a new experience of time, not as stopgap, stillness, but as *temps vierge* [virgin time]—not a blank to be filled or an untouched space to be conquered and violated, but a space which can enjoy its own potentialities and hopes—and its own presence to itself. One's *own* time. But not dominated by one's own ego and its demands. Hence open to others—compassionate time, rooted in the sense of common illusion and in criticism of it.

There is in us an instinct for newness, for renewal, for a liberation of creative power. We seek to awaken in ourselves a force which really changes our lives from within. And yet the same instinct tells us that this change is a recovery of that which is deepest, most original, most personal in ourselves. To be born again is not to become somebody else, *but to become ourselves*.

The rebirth of which Christ speaks is not a single event but a continuous dynamic of inner renewal. Certainly, sacramental baptism, the "birth by water," can be given only once. But birth in the Spirit happens many times in a man's life, as he passes through successive stages of spiritual development. A false and superficial view of Christianity assumes that it is enough to be baptized with water and to observe certain ethical and ritual prescriptions in order to guarantee for oneself a happy life in the other world. But this is only a naïve view of Christianity. True Christianity is growth in the life of the Spirit, a deepening of the new life, a continuous rebirth, in which the exterior and superficial life of the ego-self is discarded like an old snake skin and the mysterious, invisible self of the Spirit becomes more present and active. The true Christian rebirth is a renewed transformation, a "passover" in which man is progressively liberated from selfishness and not only grows in love but in some sense "becomes love." The perfection of the new birth is reached where there is no more selfishness, there is only love. In the language of the mystics there is no more selfishness, there is only love. The perfect illumination is then the illumination of Love shining by itself.

The argument between Christ and Nicodemus is renewed in every century. Each age has the answer of Nicodemus: "How can a man be born again? How can he enter again into his mother's womb?" In other words, every age has the official ideological answers that seek to evade the necessity of the divine birth. The human birth is enough: then one need only seek a political, or ethical, or doctrinal, or philosophical answer. Or one needs only to seek a new drug, a new pleasure, a new love affair, a new experience. Even the Christians themselves have at times followed Nicodemus rather than Christ, when they have identified Christianity with a given social or political or economic structure, or with a mere ideological system. But whenever a certain group of Christians has done this, then others, strangers and new converts, have come with answers to the call of the Spirit. These others have been more attentive to the quiet secret voice speaking softly in the wind. They have been willing to risk everything in order to be born again, not in the flesh but in God.

This way of wisdom is no dream, no temptation and no evasion, for it is on the contrary a return to reality in its very root. It is not an escape from contradiction and confusion for it finds unity and clarity by plunging into the very midst of contradiction, by the acceptance of emptiness and suffering, by the renunciation of passions and obsessions with which the whole world is "on fire." It does not withdraw from the fire. It is in the very heart of the fire, yet remains cool, because it has the gentleness and humility that come from self-abandonment, and hence does not seek to assert the illusion of the exterior self.

Once a man has set his foot on this way, there is no excuse for abandoning it, for to be actually on the way is to recognize without doubt or hesitation that only the way is fully real and that everything else is deception, except insofar as it may in some secret and hidden manner be connected with "the way."

Thus, far from wishing to abandon this way, the author seeks only to travel further and further along it. This journey without maps leads him into rugged mountainous country where there are often mists and storms and where he is more and more alone. Yet at the same time, ascending the slopes in darkness, feeling more and more keenly his own emptiness . . . he meets at times other travelers on the way, poor pilgrim as he is, and as solitary as he, belonging perhaps to other lands and other traditions. There are of course great differences between them, and yet they have much in common. Indeed, the author of this book [*Seeds of Contemplation*] can say that he feels himself much closer to the Zen monks of ancient Japan than to the busy and impatient men of the West, of his own country, who think in terms of money, power, publicity, machines, business, political advantage, military strategy—who seek, in a word, the triumphant affirmation of their own will, their own power, considered as the end for which they exist. Is not this perhaps the most foolish of all dreams, the most tenacious and damaging of illusions?

The mission of the contemplative in this world of massive conflict and collective unreason is to seek the true way of unity and peace, without succumbing to the illusion of withdrawing into a realm of abstraction from which unpleasant realities are simply excluded by the force of will. In facing the world with a totally different viewpoint, the contemplative maintains alive in the world the presence of a spiritual and intelligent consciousness which is the root of true peace and true unity among men. This consciousness certainly accepts the fact of our empirical and individual existence, but refuses to take this as the basic reality.

Man must believe in something, and that in which he believes becomes his god. To serve some material or human entity as one's god is to be a slave of that which perishes, and thus to be a slave of death, sorrow, falsehood, misery. The only true liberty is in the service of that which is beyond all limits, beyond all definitions, beyond all human appreciation: that which is All, and which therefore is no limited or individual thing: the All is no-thing, for if it were to be a single thing separated from all other things, it would not be All. This is precisely the liberty I have always sought: the freedom of being subject to no-thing and therefore to live in All, through All, for All, by Him who is All. In Christian terms, this is to live "in Christ" and by the "Spirit of Christ," for the Spirit is like the wind, blowing where He pleases, and He is the Spirit of Truth. "The Truth shall make you free" [John 8:32].

Man has a responsibility to his own time, not as if he could seem to stand outside it and donate various spiritual and material benefits to it from a position of compassionate distance. Man has a responsibility to find himself where he is, namely in his own proper time and in his place, in the history to which he belongs and to which he must inevitably contribute either his response or his evasions, either truth and act, or mere slogan and gesture.

I believe the major message in these pages [*Obras Completas I,* 1960] is that the contemplative life applies wherever there is life. Wherever man and society exist; where there are hopes, ideals, aspirations for a better future; where there is love—and where there is mingled pain and happiness—there the contemplative life has a place, because life, happiness, pain, ideals, aspirations, work, art and other things have significance. If these things have no significance, why waste our time on them? But, if they have significance, then the independent significance of each must converge in some way into a central and universal significance which comes from a hidden reality. This central reality has to be a "catholic" reality, a "divine" reality. The reality central to my life is the life of God. To know this is the contemplative's objective.

Can contemplation still find a place in the world of technology and conflict which is ours? Does it belong only to the past? The answer to this is that, since the direct and pure experience of reality in its ultimate root is man's deepest need, contemplation must be possible if man is to remain human. If contemplation is no longer possible, then man's life has lost the spiritual orientation upon which everything else—order, peace, happiness, sanity—must depend. But true contemplation is an austere and exacting vocation. Those who seek it are few and those who find it fewer still. Nevertheless, their presence bears witness to the fact that contemplation remains both necessary and possible.

One entered the contemplative life by making a list of things which you were going to drop, so to speak. You took the world and all its possibilities and you just crossed everything off the list. You crossed off the joys of human love; you crossed off the joys of art, music, secular literature, enjoyment of the beauties of nature, enjoyment of natural recreation, sports, swimming. All these things, you just discarded: and when you had crossed everything off the list then the one great thing was left, the *unum necessarium,* the one thing necessary!

I think we have to radically reevaluate our whole view of this "one thing necessary." The one thing necessary is not that which is left when everything is crossed off, but is perhaps that which includes and embraces everything else, that which is arrived at when you've added up everything and gone far beyond . . . . You were supposed to end up, not with what was *most* but with what was *best.* I think we should aim for the most as well as the best but not the most and the best *outside* ourselves. The most and best *in* ourselves.

I s the contemplative life to be considered a state of interior recollection and an affective absorption in God considered as Infinite Love, or is it a response to the concrete *Word of God* manifesting to us His will and His love not only for ourselves as individuals but for the whole family of man redeemed by the cross of Christ? Is our love of God to take the form of blissful repose in consolation and inner peace, or is it a total response which draws us out of ourselves beyond all concern over how we happen to *feel?* Is the contemplative life merely a cult of ordered serenity, or is it complete self-forgetfulness in obedience to God? Is the contemplative life merely to escape from the troubles and conflicts of the world to a condition of security and peace in which we "rest" and "taste" the consolations of intimacy with God? Or does it mean sharing the anguish and hope of a world in crisis in which millions struggle for the barest essentials of human existence?

Contemplation is also a response to a call: a call from Him Who has no voice, and yet Who speaks in everything that is, and Who, most of all, speaks in the depths of our own being: for we ourselves are words of His. But we are words that are meant to respond to Him, to answer Him, to echo Him, and even in some way to contain Him and signify Him. Contemplation is this echo. It is a deep resonance in the inmost center of our spirit in which our very life loses its separate voice and resounds with the majesty and mercy of the Hidden and Living One.

Therefore, most honorable reader, it is not as an author that I would speak to you, not as a story-teller, not as a philosopher, not as a friend only: I seek to speak to you, in some way, as your own self. Who can tell what this may mean? I myself do not know. But if you listen, things will be said that are perhaps not written in this book. And this will be due not to me, but to One who lives and speaks in us both!

3 | CONTEMPLATIVE LISTENING

No writing on the solitary,

meditative dimensions of life

can say anything that has not already been

said better by the wind in the pine trees.

"HONORABLE READER": REFLECTIONS ON MY WORK

ontemplation is essentially a listening in silence, an expectancy. . . . In other words, the true contemplative is not the one who prepares his mind for a particular message that he wants or expects to hear, but who remains empty because he knows that he can never expect or anticipate the word that will transform his darkness into light. He does not even anticipate a special kind of transformation. He does not demand light instead of darkness. He waits on the Word of God in silence, and when he is "answered," it is not so much by a word that bursts into his silence. It is by his silence itself suddenly, inexplicably revealing itself to him as a word of great power, full of the voice of God.

At the center of our being is a point of nothingness which is untouched by sin and by illusion, a point of pure truth, a point or spark which belongs entirely to God, which is never at our disposal, from which God disposes of our lives, which is inaccessible to the fantasies of our own mind or the brutalities of our own will. This little point of nothingness and *absolute poverty* is the pure glory of God in us. It is, so to speak, His name written in us—as our poverty, our indigence, as our dependence, as our sonship. It is like a pure diamond, blazing with the invisible light of heaven. It is in everybody, and if we could see it we would see these billion points of light coming together in the face and blaze of a sun that would make all the darkness and cruelty of life vanish completely. . . I have no program for this seeing. It is only given. But the gate of heaven is everywhere.

In those who are most alive and therefore most themselves, the life of the body is subordinated to a higher life that is in them. It quietly surrenders to the far more abundant vitality of a spirit living on the levels that defy measurement and observation. The mark of true life in man is therefore not turbulence but control, not effervescence but lucidity and direction, not passion but the sobriety that sublimates all passions and elevates it to the clear inebriation of wisdom. The control we mean here is not arbitrary and tyrannical control by an interior principle which can be called, variously, a "super-ego" or a pharisaical conscience: it is the harmonious coordination of man's power in striving for realization of his deepest spiritual potentialities. It is not so much a control of one part of man by another, but the peaceful integration of all man's powers into one perfect actuality which is his true self, that is to say, his spiritual self.

Man, then, can only fully be said to be alive when he becomes plainly conscious of the real meaning of his own existence, that is to say, when he *experiences* something of the fullness of intelligence, freedom and spirituality that are actualized within him.

What am I? I am myself a word spoken by God. Can God speak a word that does not have any meaning?

Yet am I sure that the meaning of my life is the meaning God intends for it? Does God impose a meaning on my life from the *outside,* through event, custom, routine, law, system, impact with others in society? Or am I called to create from *within,* with Him, with His grace, a meaning which reflects His truth and makes me His "word" spoken freely in my personal situation? My true identity lies hidden in God's call to my freedom and my response to him. This means I must use my freedom in order to love, with full responsibility and authenticity, not merely receiving a form imposed on me by external forces, or forming my own life according to an approved social pattern, but directing my love to the personal reality of my neighbor, and embracing God's will in its naked, often impenetrable mystery (Romans 11:33–36). I cannot discover my "meaning" if I try to evade the dread which comes from first experiencing my meaninglessness!

By meditation I penetrate the inmost ground of my life, seek the full understanding of God's will for me, of God's mercy to me, of my absolute dependence upon Him. But this penetration must be authentic. It must be something genuinely *lived* by me.

In the language of the monastic fathers, all prayer, reading, meditation and all the activities of the monastic life are aimed at *purity of heart,* an unconditional and totally humble surrender to God, a total acceptance of ourselves and of our situation as willed by Him. It means the renunciation of all deluded images of ourselves, all exaggerated estimates of our own capacities, in order to obey God's will as it comes to us in the difficult demands of life in its exacting truth. Purity of heart is then correlative to a new spiritual identity—the "self" as recognized in the context of realities willed by God. Purity of heart is the enlightened awareness of the new man, as opposed to the complex and perhaps rather disreputable fantasies of the "old man."

Meditation is then ordered to this new insight, this direct knowledge of the self in its higher aspect.

In the "prayer of the heart" we seek first of all the deepest ground of our identity in God. We do not reason about dogmas of faith, or "the mysteries." We seek rather to gain a direct existential grasp, a personal experience of the deepest truths of life and faith, *finding ourselves in God's truth*. Inner certainty depends on *purification*. The dark night rectifies our deepest intentions. In the silence of this "night of faith" [John of the Cross] we return to simplicity and sincerity of heart. We learn *recollection* which consists in listening for God's will, in direct and simple attention to *reality*. Recollection is awareness of the unconditional. *Prayer* then means yearning for the simple presence of God, for a personal understanding of His word, for knowledge of His will and for the capacity to hear and obey Him.

The kind of prayer we here speak of as properly "monastic" (though it may also fit into the life of any layperson who is attracted to it) is a prayer of silence, simplicity, contemplative and meditative unity, a deep personal integration in an attentive, watchful listening of "the heart." The response such prayer calls forth is not usually one of jubilation or audible witness: it is a word-less and total surrender of the heart in silence.

This is precisely the monk's chief service to the world: this silence, this listening, this questioning, this humble and courageous exposure to what the world ignores about itself—both good and evil.

God is known when He is apprehended as unknown, and He is heard when we realize that we do not know the sound of His voice. The words He utters are words full of silence, and they are bait to draw us into silence. The truths He manifests are full of hiddenness, and their function is to hide us, with themselves, in God from Whom they proceed. If we hide the precepts of His wisdom in our heart—precepts of humility, meekness, charity, renunciation, faith, prayer—they themselves will hide us in Him. For the values which these virtues communicate to us, the life which they give to us, are completely hidden from the eyes of men. They bring us to the source of a life that is unknown to the natural wisdom of man, and yet from this source Man's nature itself proceeds, is nourished and sustained. Thus the hidden things that are communicated to us in the words and precepts of the Gospel transform our lives and raise them from the level of distinct knowledge and clear evidence, natural prudence and plain practicality, to another level which is hidden and obscure to the mind of man.

If individualism and subjectivism are so widely suspect among us, there is perhaps a very good reason for it. We live in a climate of individualism. But our individualism is in decay. Our tradition of freedom which, as a matter of fact, is rooted in a deeply Christian soil, and which in itself is worthy of the highest respect and loyalty, has begun to lose its genuine vitality. It is becoming more and more a verbal convention rather than a spiritual conviction. The tendency to substitute words about freedom for the reality of freedom itself has brought us to a state of ambivalent spiritual servitude. The noise with which we protest our love of freedom tends to be proportionate to our actual fear of genuine freedom, and our guilt at our unconscious refusal to pay the price of freedom. The agitated and querulous license with which we abandon ourselves to our own fantasies is a purely subjective and fallacious excuse for freedom.

The illusory character of the freedom which we have tried to find in moral and psychological irresponsibility has become inescapable. Our abdication of responsibility is at the same time an abdication of liberty. The resolution to let "someone else," the anonymous forces of society, assume responsibility for everything means that we abdicate from public responsibility, from mature concern, and even from spiritual life. We retire from the public realm of freedom into the private world of necessity, imagining that the escape from responsibility is an escape into freedom. On the contrary, it is, in Erich Fromm's words, an "escape *from* freedom." But when we turn over the running of our lives to anonymous forces, to "them" (whoever "they" may be, and nobody quite knows), what actually happens is that we fall under the tyranny of collective fantasies and delusions. There is no more tyrannical dictator than convention, fashion and prejudice.

What is the real root of personality in man? It is obviously that which is *irreplaceable*, genuinely unique, on the deepest spiritual level. *Personalism* is the discovery, the respect, but not the cult, for this deep reality. Secular personalism is a kind of craze for individuality, a rage for self-manifestation in which the highest value is sought in the *recognition* by others of one's own uniqueness.

Christian personalism is, then, the sacramental sharing of the inner secret of personality in the mystery of love. This sharing demands full respect for the mystery of the person, whether it be our own person, or the person of our neighbor, or the infinite secret of God. In fact, Christian personalism is the discovery of one's own inmost self, and of the inmost self of one's neighbor, in the mystery of Christ: a discovery that respects the hiddenness and incommunicability of each one's personal secret, while paying tribute to His presence in the common celebration.

"What shall a man give in exchange for his soul?" That sentence is the very heart of Christian personalism. Our soul is irreplaceable, it can be exchanged for *nothing* in heaven or on earth, but until we have heard Christ speak, until we have received His call from the midst of the Christian Assembly (every vocation to the faith comes at least implicitly through the Church) and until we have given to Him that secret and unique answer which no one can pronounce in our place, until we have thus found ourselves in Him, we cannot fully realize what it means to be a "person" in the deepest sense of the word.

The man of faith who has never experienced doubt is not a man of faith. Consequently, the monk is one who has to struggle in the depths of his being with the presence of doubt, and to go through what some religions call the Great Doubt, to break through beyond doubt into a certitude which is very, very deep because it is not his own personal certitude; it is the certitude of God Himself, in us. The only ultimate reality is God. God lives and dwells in us. We are not justified by any action of our own, but we are called by the voice of God, by the voice of ultimate being, to pierce through the irrelevance of our life, while accepting and admitting that our life is totally irrelevant, in order to find relevance in Him. And this relevance in Him is not something we can grasp or possess. It is something that can only be received as a gift. Consequently, the kind of life that I represent is a life that is openness to gift: gift from God and gift from others.

Underlying all life is the ground of doubt and self-questioning which sooner or later must bring us face to face with the ultimate meaning of our life. This self-questioning can never be without a certain existential "dread"—a sense of insecurity, of "lostness," of exile, of sin. A sense that one has somehow been untrue not so much to abstract moral or social norms but to one's inmost truth. "Dread" in this sense is not simply a foolish childhood fear of retribution, or a naïve guilt, a fear of violating taboos. It is the profound awareness that one is capable of an ultimate bad faith with himself and with others: that one is living a lie.

Growth in experience implies a serious self-doubt and self-questioning in which values previously held seem to be completely exploded and no other tangible values come to take their place. This may even take the form of a crisis of religious faith in which our whole conception of God and of our relationship to Him may be turned upside down. There may seem to be "no God" at all, or else our relationship to Him may seem so desperate that we feel as though we are damned, in our moments of darkness. This, as St. John of the Cross shows, marks the beginning of a whole new experience of faith on a completely different level. The passage from a state in which one loves and worships God as a beautiful object of desire to a state in which God ceases to be object and loses all definite limitations in our mind is something which cannot be easily described: but it is a perilous, though necessary, experience.

Dread is an expression of our insecurity in this earthly life, a realization that we are never and can never be completely "sure" in the sense of possessing a definitive and established spiritual status. It means that we cannot any longer hope in ourselves, in our wisdom, our virtues, our fidelity. We see too clearly that all that is "ours" is nothing, and can completely fail us. In other words we no longer rely on what we "have," what has been given by our past, what has been required. We are open to God and to His mercy in the inscrutable future and our trust in the emptiness where we will confront unforeseen decisions. Only when we have descended in the dread to the center of our own nothingness, by His grace and His guidance, can we be led by Him, in His own time, to find Him in losing ourselves.

My Lord God, I have no idea where I am going. I do not see the road ahead of me. I cannot know for certain where it will end. Nor do I really know myself, and the fact that I think I am following Your will does not mean that I am actually doing so. But I believe that the desire to please You does in fact please You. And I hope I have that desire in all that I am doing. I hope that I will never do anything apart from that desire. And I know that if I do this You will lead me by the right road, though I may know nothing about it. Therefore I will trust You always though I may seem to be lost and in the shadow of death. I will not fear, for You are ever with me, and You will never leave me to face my perils alone.

4 | DIALOGUING WITH SILENCE

Let me seek, then, the gift of silence,

and poverty, and solitude

where everything I touch is turned into a prayer:

where the sky is my prayer, the birds are my

prayer,the wind in the trees is my prayer,

for God is all in all.

THOUGHTS IN SOLITUDE

God is present, and His thought is alive and awake in the fullness and depth and breadth of all the silences of the world. The Lord is watching in the almond trees, over the fulfillment of His words (Jeremias 1:11).

Whether the plane passes by tonight or tomorrow, whether there be cars on the winding road or no cars, whether men speak in the field, whether there be a radio in the house or not, the tree brings forth her blossoms in silence.

Whether the house be empty or full of children, whether the men go off to town or work with tractors in the fields, whether the liner enters the harbor full of tourists or full of soldiers, the almond tree brings forth her fruit in silence.

There must be a time of day when the man who makes plans forgets his plans, and acts as if he had no plans at all.

There must be a time of day when the man who has to speak falls very silent. And his mind forms no more propositions, and he asks himself: Did they have a meaning?

There must be a time when the man of prayer goes to pray as if it were the first time in his life he had ever prayed; when the man of resolutions puts his resolutions aside as if they had all been broken, and he learns a different wisdom: distinguishing the sun from the moon, the stars from the darkness, the sea from dry land, and the night sky from the shoulder of a hill.

There is not much use talking to men about God and love if they are not able to listen. The ears with which one hears the message of the Gospel are hidden in man's heart, and these ears do not hear anything unless they are favored with a certain interior solitude and silence.

Those who love their own noise are impatient of everything else. They constantly defile the silence of the forests and the mountains and the sea. They bore through silent nature in every direction with their machines, for fear that the calm world might accuse them of their own emptiness. The urgency of their swift movement seems to ignore the tranquility of nature by pretending to have a purpose. The loud plane seems for a moment to deny the reality of the clouds and of the sky, by its direction, its noise, and its pretended strength. The silence of the sky remains when the plane has gone. The tranquility of the clouds will remain when the plane has fallen apart. It is the silence of the world that is real. Our noise, our business, our purposes, and all our fatuous statements about our purposes, our business, and our noise: these are the illusion.

It is not speaking that breaks our silence, but the anxiety to be heard. The words of the proud man impose silence on all others, so that he alone may be heard. The humble man speaks only in order to be spoken to. The humble man asks nothing but an alms, then waits and listens.

If there is no silence beyond and within the words of doctrine, there is no religion, only religious ideology. For religion goes beyond words and actions, and attains to the ultimate truth in silence. When this silence is lacking, where there are only the "many words" and not the One Word, then there is much bustle and activity, but no peace, no deep thought, no understanding, no inner quiet. Where there is no peace, there is no light. The mind that is hyperactive seems to itself to be awake and productive, but it is dreaming. Only in silence and solitude, in the quiet of worship, the reverent peace of prayer, the adoration in which the entire ego-self silences and abases itself in the presence of the Invisible God, only in these "activities" which are "non-actions" does the spirit truly awake from the dream of a multifarious and confused existence.

The message of God's mercy to man must be preached. The word of truth must be proclaimed. No one can deny this. But there are not a few who are beginning to feel the futility of adding more words to the constant flood of language that pours meaninglessly over everybody, everywhere, from morning to night. For language to have meaning there must be intervals of silence somewhere, to divide word from word and utterance from utterance. He who retires into silence does not necessarily hate language. Perhaps it is love and respect for language which imposes silence upon him. For the mercy of God is not heard in words unless it is heard, both before and after the words are spoken, in silence.

Is it true to say that one goes into solitude to get at the root of existence? It would be better to say that in solitude one *is* at the root. He who is alone, and is conscious of what his solitude means, finds himself simply in the ground of life. He is not surprised at it, and he is able to live with this disconcerting and unexciting reality, which has no explanation. He lives, then, as a seed planted in the ground. As Christ said, the seed in the ground must die. To be as a seed in the ground of one's very life is to dissolve in that ground in order to become fruitful. But this fruitfulness is beyond any planning and any understanding of man. To be "fruitful" in this sense, one must forget every idea of fruitfulness or productivity, and merely *be*. One's fruitfulness is at once an act of faith and an act of doubt: doubt of all that one has hitherto seen in oneself, and faith in what one cannot possibly imagine for oneself. The "doubt" dissolves our ego-identity.

F aith gives us life in Christ, according to St. Paul's word: "I live, now not I, but Christ lives in me" (Galatians 2:20). To accept this is impossible unless one has profound hope in the incomprehensible fruitfulness that emerges from this dissolution of our ego in the ground of our being. Such hope is not the product of human reason; it is a secret gift of grace. It sustains us with divine and hidden aid. To accept our own dissolution would be inhuman if we did not at the same time accept the wholeness and completeness of everything in God. We accept our emptying because we realize that our very emptiness is fulfillment and plenitude. In our emptiness the One Word is clearly spoken.

As soon as a man is fully disposed to be alone with God, he is alone with God no matter where he may be—in the country, the monastery, the woods, or the city. The lightning flashes from east to west, illuminating the whole horizon and striking where it pleases, and at the same instant the infinite liberty of God flashes in the depths of the man's soul and he is illumined. At that moment he sees that though he seems to be in the middle of his journey, he has already arrived at the end. For the life of grace on earth is the beginning of the life of glory. Although he is a traveler in time, he has opened his eyes, for a moment, in eternity.

The solitary is one who is called to make one of the most terrible decisions possible to man: the decision to disagree completely with those who imagine that the call to diversion and self-deception is the voice of truth and who can summon the full authority of their own prejudice to prove it. He is therefore bound to sweat blood in anguish in order to be loyal to God, to the Mystical Christ, and to humanity as a whole, rather than to the idol which is offered to him, for his homage, by a particular group. He must renounce the blessing of every convenient illusion that absolves him from responsibility when he is untrue to his deepest self and to his inmost truth—the image of God in his own soul.

The price of fidelity in such a task is a completely dedicated humility—an emptiness of heart in which self-assertion has no place. For, if he is not empty and undivided in his own inmost soul, the solitary will be nothing more than an individualist. And in that case, his non-conformity is nothing but an act of rebellion: the substitution of idols and illusions of his own choosing for those chosen by society.

Without solitude of some sort there is and can be no maturity. Unless one becomes empty and alone, he cannot give himself in love because he does not possess the deep self which is the only gift worthy of love. And this deep self, we immediately add, cannot be *possessed*. My deep self is not "something" which I acquire, or to which I "attain" after a long struggle. It is not mine, and cannot become mine. It is no "thing"—no object. It is "I."

The shallow "I" of individualism can be possessed, developed, cultivated, pandered to, satisfied: it is the center of all our strivings for gain and for satisfaction, whether material or spiritual. But the deep "I" of the spirit, of solitude and love, cannot be "had," possessed, developed, perfected. It can only be, and act according to deep inner laws which are not of man's contriving, but which come from God. They are the Laws of the Spirit, who, like the wind, blows where He wills [John 3:8]. This inner "I," who is always alone, is always universal: for in this inmost "I" my own solitude meets the solitude of every other man and the solitude of God.

In an age when totalitarianism has striven, in every way, to devaluate and degrade the human person, we hope it is right to demand a hearing for any and every sane reaction in favor of man's inalienable solitude and his interior freedom. The murderous din of our materialism cannot be allowed to silence the independent voices which will never cease to speak: whether they be the voices of Christian saints, or the voices of Oriental sages like Lao-Tse or the Zen Masters, or the voices of men like Thoreau or Martin Buber or Max Picard. It is all very well to insist that man is a "social animal"—the fact is obvious enough. But there is no justification for making him a mere cog in a totalitarian machine—or in a religious one either, for that matter.

Man is a rational animal, they say. But he does not exist merely in order to grow, or eat, or work, or think, or even to love. On the contrary, growth, nutrition, work, thought and love all unite in promoting and increasing the existential depth of that mysterious reality which is the individual person, a concrete, free, inexplicable being endowed with powers whose depth no mind but God's can ever fathom. The human person, then, is a free being created with capacities that can only be fulfilled by the vision of an unknown God. And the monk is a person who has been unable to resist the need to seek this unknown God in the hiddenness and silence of His own inscrutable wisdom.

Hard as it is to convey in human language, there is a very real and very recognizable (but almost entirely indefinable) presence of God, in which we confront Him in prayer knowing Him by Whom we are known, aware of Him Who is aware of us, loving Him by Whom we know ourselves to be loved. Present to ourselves in the fullness of our own personality, we are present to Him Who is infinite in His Being, His Otherness, His Self-hood. It is not a vision face-to-face, but a certain presence of self to Self in which, with the reverent attention of our whole being, we know Him in Whom all things have their being. The "eye" which opens to His presence is in the very center of our humility, in the very heart of our freedom, in the very depths of our spiritual nature. Meditation is the opening of this eye.

Vocation to Solitude—to deliver oneself up, to hand oneself over, entrust oneself completely to the silence of a wide landscape of woods and hills, or sea, or desert; to sit still while the sun comes up over that land and fills its silences with light. To pray and work in the morning, and to labor and rest in the afternoon, and to sit still again in meditation in the evening when night falls upon that land and when the silence fills itself with darkness and with stars. This is a true and special vocation. There are few who are willing to belong completely to such silence, to let it soak into their bones, to breathe nothing but silence, to feed on silence, and to turn the very substance of their life into a living and vigilant silence.

The vocation to solitude is therefore at the same time a vocation to silence, poverty and emptiness. But the emptiness is for the sake of fullness: the purpose of the solitary life is, if you like, contemplation. But not contemplation in the pagan sense of an intellectual, esoteric enlightenment, achieved by ascetic technique. The contemplation of the Christian solitary is the awareness of the divine mercy transforming and elevating his own emptiness and turning it into the presence of perfect love, perfect fullness.

Some will seek clarity in isolation and silence, not because they think they know better than the rest, but because they want to see life in a different perspective. They want to withdraw from the Babel of confusion in order to listen more patiently to the voice of their conscience and to the Holy Spirit. And by their prayers and their fidelity they will invisibly renew the life of the whole Church. This renewal will communicate itself to others who remain "in the world" and will help them also to regain a clearer vision, a sharper and more promising appreciation of Christian truth. These will give themselves to apostolic work on a new level of seriousness and of faith. They will be able to discard fictitious gestures of zeal in favor of genuine self-sacrificing love.

So when, as in our time, the whole world seems to have become one immense and idiotic fiction, and when the virus of mendacity creeps into every vein and organ of the social body, it would be abnormal and immoral if there were no reaction. It is even healthy that the reaction should sometimes take the form of outspoken protest, as long as we remember that solitude is no refuge for the rebellious.

And if there is an element of protest in the solitary vocation, the element must be a matter of rigorous spirituality. It must be deep and interior, and intimately personal, so that the solitary is one who is critical, first of all, of himself. Otherwise he will divert himself with a fiction worse than that of all the others, becoming a more insane and self-opinionated liar than the worst of them, cheating no one more than himself. Solitude is not for rebels like this, and it promptly rejects them. The desert is for those who have felt a salutary despair of conventional and fictitious values, in order to hope in mercy and to be themselves merciful men to whom that mercy is promised. Such solitaries know the evils that are in other men because they experience these evils first of all in themselves.

Such men, out of pity for the universe, out of loyalty to mankind, and without a spirit of bitterness or of resentment, withdraw into the healing silence of the wilderness, or of poverty, or of obscurity, not in order to preach to others but to heal in themselves the wounds of the entire world.

The greatest of God's secrets is God Himself.

He waits to communicate Himself to me in a way that I can never express to others or even think about coherently to myself. I must desire it in silence. It is for this that I must leave all things.

My life is a listening; His is a speaking. My salvation is to hear and respond. For this, my life must be silent. Hence, my silence is my salvation.

To be one with One Whom one cannot see is to be hidden, to be nowhere, to be no one: it is to be unknown as He is unknown, forgotten as He is forgotten, lost as He is lost to the world which nevertheless exists in Him. Yet to live in Him is to live by His power, to reach from end to end of the universe in the might of His wisdom, to rule and form all things in and with Him. It is to be the hidden instrument of His Divine action, the minister of His redemption, the channel of His mercy, and the messenger of His infinite Love.

The victory of monastic humility is the full acceptance of God's hidden action in the weakness and ordinariness and unsatisfactoriness of our own everyday lives. It is the acceptance of our own incompleteness, in order that He may make us complete in His own way. It is joy in our emptiness, which can only be filled by Him. It is peace in our own unfruitfulness which He Himself makes immensely fruitful without our being able to understand how it is done.

5 | THE INNER EXPERIENCE OF LOVE

If you want a spiritual life, you must unify your

life. A life is either all spiritual or not at all.

No man can serve two masters.

Your life is shaped by the end you live for.

You are made in the image of what you desire.

THOUGHTS IN SOLITUDE

Man in our day, menaced on all sides with ruin, is at the same time beset with illusory promises of happiness. Both threat and promise often come from the same political source. Both hell and heaven have become, so they say, immediate possibilities here on earth. It is true that the emotional hell and heaven which each one of us carries about within him tend to become more and more public and common property. And, as time goes on, it seems evident that what we have to share seems to be not so much one another's heaven as one another's hell.

It is well known that in the Orient, in China, India, Japan, and Indonesia, the religious and contemplative life has been fostered for centuries and has known a development of unparalleled richness. Asia has for centuries been a continent of great monastic communities. At the same time the solitary life has flourished, either in the shadow of the monasteries or in the wilderness of jungle, mountain, or desert. Hindu yoga, in its various forms, has become almost legendary of Eastern contemplation. Yoga makes use of a variety of disciplines and ascetic techniques for the "liberation" of man's spirit from the limitations imposed upon him by material, bodily existence. Everywhere in the East, whether in Hinduism or Buddhism, we find that deep, unutterable thirst for the rivers of Paradise. Whatever may be the philosophies and theologies behind these forms of contemplative existence, the striving is always the same: the quest for unity, a return to the inmost self united with the Absolute, a quest for Him Who is above all, and in all, and Who Alone is Alone.

The great practitioners of contemplation, the Desert Fathers of Egypt and the Near East, did their best to dispel the illusion [of contemplation as a life of ease, aestheticism and speculation]. They went into the desert not to seek pure spiritual beauty or an intellectual light, but to see the Face of God. And they knew that before they could see His Face, they would have to struggle, instead, with His adversary. They would have to cast out the devil subtly lodged in their exterior self. They went into the desert not to study speculative truth, but to wrestle with practical evil; not to perfect their analytical intelligence, but to purify their hearts. They went into solitude not to *get* something, but in order to *give themselves,* for "He that would save his life must lose it, and he that would lose his life, for the sake of Christ, shall save it" [Matthew 16:25]. By their renunciation of passion and attachment, their crucifixion of the exterior self, they liberated the inner man, the new man "in Christ."

The important thing in contemplation is not enjoyment, not pleasure, not happiness, not peace, but the transcendent experience of reality and truth in the act of supreme and liberated spiritual love. The important thing in contemplation is not gratification and rest, but awareness, life, creativity, and freedom. In fact, contemplation is man's highest and most essential spiritual activity. It is his most creative and dynamic affirmation of his divine sonship. It is not just the sleepy, suave, restful embrace of "being" in a dark, generalized contentment: it is a flash of lightning of divinity piercing the darkness of nothingness and sin. Not something general and abstract, but something, on the contrary, as concrete, particular, and "existential" as it can possibly be. It is the confrontation of man with his God, of the Son with His Father. It is the awakening of Christ within us, the establishment of the Kingdom of God in our own soul, the triumph of the Truth and of Divine Freedom in the inmost "I" in which the Father becomes one with the Son in the Spirit Who is given to the believer.

The story of Adam's fall from Paradise says, in symbolic terms, that man was created as a contemplative. The fall from Paradise was a fall from unity . . . Man fell from the unity of contemplative vision into the multiplicity, complication, and distraction of an active, worldly existence.

Since he was not dependent entirely on exterior and contingent things, he became an exile in a world of objects, each one capable of deluding and enslaving him. Centered no longer on God and in his inmost, spiritual self, man now had to *see* and *be aware* of himself as if he were his own god. He had to study himself as a kind of pseudo-object, from which he was estranged. And to compensate for the labors and frustrations of this estrangement, he must try to admire, assert and gratify himself at the expense of others like himself. Hence the complex and painful network of loves and hatreds, desires and fears, lies and excuses in which we are all held captive. In such a condition, man's mind is enslaved by an inexorable concern with all that is exterior, transient, illusory and trivial. And carried away by his pursuit of alien shadows and forms, he can no longer see his own true inner "face," or recognize his identity in the spirit an in God, for that identity is secret, invisible and incommunicable. But man has lost the courage and the faith without which he cannot be content to be "unseen." He is pitifully dependent on self-observation and self-assertion. That is to say, he is utterly exiled from God and from his own true self, for neither in God nor in our inmost self can there be any aggressive self-assertion: there is only the plain presence of love and of truth.

Man is exiled from God and from his inmost self. He is tempted to seek God, and happiness, outside himself. So his quest for happiness becomes, in fact, a flight from God and from himself: a flight that takes him further and further away from reality. In the end, he has to dwell in the "region of unlikeness"—having lost his inner resemblance to God in losing his freedom to enter his own home, which is the sanctuary of God.

But man must return to Paradise. He must recover himself, salvage his dignity, recollect his lost wits, and return to his true identity. There is only one way in which this could be done, says the Gospel of Christ. God Himself must come, like the woman in the parable seeking the lost groat [penny]. God Himself must become Man, in order that, in the Man-God, man might be able to lose himself as man and find himself as God.

hristianity is life and wisdom in Christ. It is a return to the Father in Christ. It is a return to the infinite abyss of pure reality in which our own reality is grounded, and in which we exist. It is a return to the source of all meaning and truth. It is a return to the inmost springs of life and joy. It is a rediscovery of paradise within our own spirit by self-forgetfulness. And, because of our oneness with Christ, it is the recognition of ourselves as sons of the Father. It is the recognition of ourselves as other Christs. It is the awareness of strength and love imparted to us by the miraculous presence of the Nameless and Hidden One Whom we call the Holy Spirit.

N ow all our existence in this life is subject to change and recurrence. That alone does not make it secular. But life becomes secularized when it commits itself completely to the "cycles" of what *appears to be new,* but is in fact the same thing over again. Secular life is a life of vain hopes imprisoned in the illusion of newness and change, an illusion which brings us constantly back to the same old point, the contemplation of our own nothingness. Secular life is a life frantically dedicated to escape, through novelty and variety, from the fear of death. But the more we cherish secular hopes, the more they disappoint us. And the more they disappoint us, the more desperately do we return to the attack and forge new hopes more extravagant than the last. These too let us down. And we revert to that insufferable condition from which we have vainly tried to escape. In the words of Blaise Pascal:

Nothing is so unbearable to a man as to be completely at rest, without passions, without business, without diversion, without study. He then feels his nothingness, his falseness, his insufficiency, his dependence, his weakness, his emptiness . . . (Pensées, 131)

The truly sacred attitude toward life is in no sense an escape from the sense of nothingness that assails us when we are left alone with ourselves. On the contrary, it penetrates into that darkness and that nothingness, realizing that the mercy of God has transformed our nothingness into His temple and believing that in our darkness His light has hidden itself. Hence the sacred attitude is one which does not recoil from our own inner emptiness, but rather penetrates into it with awe and reverence, and with the awareness of mystery.

The external *self* fears and recoils from what is beyond it and above it. It dreads the seeming emptiness and darkness of the interior self. The whole tragedy of "diversion" is precisely that it is a flight from all that is most real and immediate and genuine in ourselves. It is a flight from life and from experience—an attempt to put a veil of objects between the mind and experience itself. It is therefore a matter of great courage and spiritual energy to turn away from diversion and prepare to meet, face-to-face, that *immediate* experience of life which is intolerable to the exterior man. This is only possible when, by a gift of God (St. Thomas Aquinas would say it was the Gift of Fear, or sacred awe) we are able to see our inner selves not as a vacuum but as an *infinite depth,* not as emptiness but as fullness. This change of perspective is impossible as long as we are afraid of our own nothingness, as long as we are afraid of fear, afraid of poverty, afraid of boredom—as long as we run away from ourselves.

The man whose view of life is purely secular hates himself interiorly, while seeming to love himself. He hates himself in the sense that he cannot stand to be "with" or "by" himself. And because he hates himself, he also tends to hate God, because he cannot abide the inner loneliness which must be suffered and accepted before God can be found. His rebellion against his own inner loneliness and poverty turns into pride. Pride is the fixation of the interior self upon itself and the rejection of all other elements in the self for which it is incapable of assuming responsibility. This includes the rejection of the inmost self, with its apparent emptiness, its indefiniteness, and its general character as that which is dark and unknown. Pride is, then, a false and evasive self-realization which is in actual fact no realization at all, but only the fabrication of an illusory image. The effort which must then be put into the protection and substantiation of this illusion gives the appearance of strength. But in reality this fixation upon what does not exist merely exhausts and ruins our being.

There is a subtle but inescapable connection between the "sacred" attitude and the acceptance of one's inmost self. The movement of recognition which accepts our own obscure and unknown self produces the sensation of a "numinous" presence within us. This sacred awe is no mere magic illusion, but the real expression of a release of spiritual energy, testifying to our own interior reunion and reconciliation with that which is deepest in us and, through the inner self, with the transcendent and invisible power of God. This implies humility, or the full acceptance of all that we have tended to reject and ignore in ourselves. The inner self is "purified" by the acknowledgment of sin, not precisely because the inner self is the seat of sin, but because both our sinfulness and interiority tend to be rejected in one and the same movement by the exterior self and relegated to the same darkness, so that when the inner self is brought back to light, sin emerges and is liquidated by the assuming of responsibility and by sorrow.

Thus the man with the "sacred" view is one who does not need to hate himself, and is never afraid or ashamed to remain with his own loneliness, for in it he is at peace, and through it he can come to the presence of God. More still, he is able to go out from his own loneliness to find God in other men. That is to say, in his dealings with others he has no need to identify them with their sins and condemn them for their actions, for he is able, in them also, to see below the surface and to guess at the presence of the inner and innocent self that is the image of God. Such a man is able to help other men to find God in themselves, educating them in confidence by the respect he is able to feel for them. Thus he is capable of allaying some of their fears and helping them to put up with themselves, until they become interiorly quiet and learn to see God in the depths of their own poverty.

The basic and most fundamental problem in the spiritual life is this acceptance of our hidden and dark self, with which we tend to identify all the evil that is in us. We must learn by discernment to separate the evil growth of our actions from the good ground of the soul. And we must prepare that ground so that a new life can grow up from it within us, beyond our knowledge and beyond our conscious control. The sacred attitude is then one of reverence, awe and silence before the mystery that begins to take place within us when we become aware of our inmost self. In silence, hope, expectation, and unknowing, the man of faith abandons himself to the divine will: not as to an arbitrary and magic power whose decrees must be spelled out from cryptic ciphers, but as to the stream of reality and of life itself. The sacred attitude is, then, one of deep and fundamental respect for the real in whatever new form it may present itself.

In active contemplation, there is a deliberate and sustained effort to detect the will of God in events and to bring one's whole self into harmony with that will. Active contemplation depends on an *ascesis* [an inner struggle] of abandonment, a systematic relaxation of the tensions of the exterior self and a renunciation of its tyrannical claims and demands, in order to move in a dimension that escapes our understanding and overflows in all directions our capacity to plan. The element of dialectic in active contemplation is centered on the discovery of God's will, that is to say, the identification of the real direction which events are taking, especially in our own life. But along with this there is a deep concern with the symbolic and ritual enactment of those sacred mysteries which represent the divine actions by which the redemption and sanctification of the world is effected. In other words, active contemplation rests on a deep ground of liturgical, historical, and cultural tradition: but a living tradition, not dead convention. And a tradition still in dynamic growth and movement.

The contemplative mind is, in fact, not normally ultra-conservative, but neither is it necessarily radical. It transcends both these extremes in order to remain in living contact with that which is genuinely true in any traditional movement. Hence I would say in parentheses that the contemplative mind today will not normally be associated too firmly or too definitively with any "movement," whether political, religious, liturgical, artistic, philosophical, or what have you. The contemplative stays clear of movements, not because they confuse him, but simply because he does not need them and can go farther by himself than he can in their formalized and often fanatical ranks.

Nevertheless active contemplation should be to a great extent in contact with the *logos* of its age. This means in simple fact that the contemplative today might be expected to have an intuitive grasp of and even sympathy for what is most genuine in the characteristic movements of our time—Marxism, existentialism, psychoanalysis, eirenism [efforts to achieve mental peace]. They may even at times present a serious temptation for him. But if he is a genuine contemplative, he will be able to resist temptation because his contemplation itself will instinctively avoid becoming enmeshed in conceptual systems. I say if he is a genuine contemplative, meaning "if he is sufficiently initiated into the meaning and value of a spiritual life to prefer its simplicity to all the complexities and pretenses of these intellectual fads and campaigns."

In active contemplation, a man becomes able to live within himself. He learns to be at home with his own thoughts. He becomes to a greater and greater degree independent of exterior supports. His mind is pacified not by passive dependence on things outside himself—diversions, entertainments, conversations, business—but by its own constructive activity. That is to say that he derives inner satisfaction from spiritual creativeness: thinking his own thoughts, reaching his own conclusions, looking at his own life and directing it in accordance with his own inner truth, discovered in meditation and under the eyes of God. He derives strength not from what he gets out of things and people, but from giving himself to life and to others. He discovers the secret of life in the *creative energy of love*— not love as a sentimental or sensual indulgence, but as a profound and self-oblative expression of freedom.

Contemplation should not be exaggerated, distorted, and made to seem great. It is essentially simple and humble. No one can enter into it except by the path of obscurity and self-forgetfulness. It implies also much discipline, but above all the normal discipline of everyday virtue. It implies justice to other people, truthfulness, hard work, unselfishness, devotion to the duties of one's state in life, obedience, charity, self-sacrifice. No one should delude himself with contemplative aspirations if he is not willing to undertake, first of all, the ordinary labors and obligations of the moral life. Contemplation is not a kind of magic and easy shortcut to happiness and peace. And yet it does bring one in touch with God in an I-Thou relationship of mysteriously experienced friendship; it necessarily brings that peace which Christ promised and which "the world cannot give." There may be much desolation and suffering in the spirit of the contemplative, but there is always more joy than sorrow, more security than doubt, more peace than desolation. The contemplative is one who has found what every man seeks in one way or other.

The great obstacle to contemplation is rigidity and prejudice. He who thinks he knows what it is beforehand prevents himself from finding out the true nature of contemplation, since he is not able to "change his mind" and accept something completely new. He who thinks that contemplation is lofty and spectacular cannot receive the intuition of a supreme and transcendent Reality which is at the same time in his own ordinary self. He who needs to be exalted and for whom mysticism is the peak of human ambition will never be able to feel the liberation granted only to those who have renounced success. And since most of us are rigid, attached to our own ideas, convinced of our own wisdom, proud of our own capacities, and committed to personal ambition, contemplation is a dangerous desire for any one of us. But if we really want to get free from these sins, the desire for contemplative freedom and for the experience of transcendent reality is likely to arise in us by itself, unobserved. And it is also likely to be satisfied almost before we know we have it. That is the way a genuine contemplative vocation is realized.

6 | A MONASTIC LIFE OF PRAYER AND PROTEST

Prayer is freedom and affirmation

growing out of nothingness into love.

Prayer is the flowering of our inmost freedom

in response to the Word of God.

CONTEMPLATION IN A WORLD OF ACTION

A monk has been called by the Holy Spirit to relinquish the cares, desires and ambitions of other men, and devote his entire life to seeking God. The concept is familiar. The reality which the concept signifies is a mystery. For in actual fact, no one on earth knows precisely what it means to "seek God" until he himself has set out to find Him. No man can tell another what this search means unless that other is enlightened, at the same time, by the Spirit speaking within his own heart. In the end, no one can seek God unless he has already begun to find Him. No one can find God without having first been found by Him. A monk seeks God because he has been found by God.

I have never had any doubt whatever of my monastic vocation. If I have ever had any desire for change, it has been for a more solitary, more "monastic" way. But precisely because of this it can be said that I am in some sense everywhere. My monastery is not a home. It is not a place where I am rooted and established in the earth. It is not an environment in which I become aware of myself as an individual, but rather a place in which I disappear from the world as an object of interest in order to be everywhere in it by hiddenness and compassion. To exist everywhere I have to be No-one.

The monastery is not an "escape" from the world. On the contrary, by being in the monastery I take my true part in all the struggles and sufferings of the world. To adopt a life that is essentially non-assertive, non-violent, a life of humility and peace, is in itself a statement of one's position. But each one in such a life can, by the personal modality of his decision, give his whole life a special orientation. It is my intention to make my entire life a rejection of, a protest against, the crimes and injustices of war and political tyranny which threaten to destroy the whole race of man and the world with him. By my monastic life and vows I am saying NO to all the concentration camps, the aerial bombardments, the staged political trials, the judicial murders, the racial injustices, the economic tyrannies, and the whole socioeconomic apparatus which seems geared for nothing but global destruction in spite of all its fair words in favor of peace.

I make monastic silence a protest against the lies of politicians, propagandists and agitators, and, when I speak, it is to deny that my faith and my Church can ever seriously be aligned with these forces of injustice and destruction. But it is true, nevertheless, that the faith in which I believe is also invoked by many who believe in war, believe in racial injustices, and believe in self-righteous and lying forms of tyranny. My life must, then, be a protest against these also and perhaps against these most of all.

If I say NO to all these secular forces, I also say YES to all that is good in the world and in mankind. I say YES to all that is beautiful in nature and, in order that this may be the yes of freedom and not of subjection, I must refuse to possess anything in the world purely as my own. I say YES to all the men and women who are my brothers and sisters in the world, but for this yes to be an assent of freedom and not of subjection, I must live so that no one may seem to belong to me, and that I may not belong to any of them. It is because I want to be more to them than a friend that I become, to all of them, a stranger.

To be ravished from the world of men by the silence of God means, in the end, not that one finds a new and mysterious universe to live in, but that the old, ordinary universe, with all its everyday poverty and charm, while remaining perfectly ordinary, perfectly real, perfectly poor, becomes transfigured from within by a silence which is the supreme and infinite "poverty" of an infinitely rich and generous God!

Formed by the discipline of a hidden wisdom, monks become themselves as hidden as wisdom is herself. They remain in this mortal life, and yet their life is already hidden with Christ in God and their citizenship is in heaven. They do not expect to be understood by men because they do not fully understand themselves. They realize that their silence is something of a problem and a scandal to those who happen to notice it: but they cannot fully explain the mystery to anyone. They are, themselves, too much a part of the mystery of silence to be able to formulate an apologetic for their own lives. Like wisdom, they manifest themselves by remaining hidden.

The monastic vocation is therefore by its very nature a call to the wilderness, because it is a call to live in hope. The monk carries on the long tradition of waiting and hoping, the long Advent of the patriarchs and prophets: an Advent which prolongs our expectation even though the Savior has come. For though Jesus has saved the world, the fruitful waters of those four rivers of Paradise, once more made accessible by the cross, have not yet been poured out on all mankind. Even in the souls of the baptized, there is still so much that is unfruitful, so much darkness, so much emptiness, so much barren rock. The monk leaves the world, retires to the wilderness, the forest, the mountains, the lonely shores of the sea: and there, descending by his prayer into the empty spaces of his own spirit, he waits for the fulfillment of the divine promises: "The land that was desolate and impassable shall be glad, and the wilderness shall rejoice and shall flourish like the lily" (Isaias 35:1).

The monk is a man of paradise who consecrates himself to God by a solemn and perpetual vow in order to spend his entire life in cultivating the spiritual Eden, the "new creation" of space and light marvelously affected by God through the Incarnation, Passion and Resurrection of His Son. The monk is one who, by penance and austerity, solitude, silence, renunciation, keeps himself from forgetting that the earth of his soul is "void and empty." By prayer and faith and contemplation, he preserves the "face of the abyss" which is his soul from the illusory lights of merely human wisdom, and entering with Christ into the desert, he struggles with the evil that is in the world by reason of man's sin. As Adam once received the task of cultivating Paradise and keeping it, so now the monk, strengthened by the invisible presence of Christ, takes upon himself the apparently hopeless task of cultivating the desert—the sandy wastes of the human spirit deprived of God. The Spirit hovers over the wasteland, to bring it fertility, and the Word again pitches His tent in man's world.

To properly understand prayer, we have to see in it this encounter of our freedom emerging from the depth of nothingness and undevelopment, at the call of God. Prayer is freedom and affirmation growing out of nothingness into love. Prayer is the flowering of our inmost freedom, in response to the Word of God. Prayer is not only dialogue with God: it is the communion of our freedom with His ultimate freedom, His infinite spirit. It is the elevation of our limited freedom into the infinite freedom of the divine spirit, and of the divine love. Prayer is the encounter of our freedom with the all-embracing charity which knows no limit and knows no obstacle.

Are monks and hippies and poets relevant? No, we are deliberately irrelevant. We live with an ingrained irrelevance which is proper to every human being. The marginal man accepts the basic irrelevance of the human condition, an irrelevance which is manifested above all by the very fact of death. The marginal person, the monk, the displaced person, the prisoner, all these people live in the presence of death, which calls into question the meaning of life. He struggles with the fact of death in himself, trying to seek something deeper than death, and the office of the monk or the marginal person, the meditative person or the poet, is to go beyond death even in this life, to go beyond the dichotomy of life and death and to be, therefore, a witness of life.

It is not that we go out into the world with a capacity to love others greatly. This too we know in ourselves, that our capacity to love is limited. And it has to be completed with the capacity to be loved, to accept love from others, to want to be loved by others, to admit our loneliness and to live with our loneliness because everybody is lonely. This is then another basis for the kind of experience that I am talking about, which is a new approach, a different approach to the external experience of the monk. The monk in his solitude and in his meditation seeks this dimension of life.

All the substance of the monastic vocation, therefore, is buried in the silence where God and the soul meet, not as object and subject, but as "one Spirit." The very essence of monasticism is hidden in the existential darkness of life itself. And life is inexplicable, irreducible to systematic terms. It is only understood by being lived. The best we can say is that the monk is one who goes out to the frontiers of liberty and of existence, seeking the impossible, seeking the vision which no man can see without dying. And yet this idea must immediately be corrected, for it is at once exaggerated and misleading. For when the monk is able to reach a certain degree of wisdom, he realizes that he had already found God by becoming mysteriously unwise. And then the circle is closed, and the monastic life begins.

The terrible human aspiration that reaches out over the abyss is calmed. The terror of God is so far beyond all conceivable terror that it ceases to terrify and then suddenly becomes friendly. Then, at last, begins the utterly unbelievable consolation, the consolation into which we enter through the door of an apparent despair: the deep conviction, as impossible to explain as it is to resist, that in the depths of our uselessness and futility we are one with God. "He who is joined to the Lord in one spirit." We have found Him in the abyss of our own poverty—not in a horrible night, not in a tragic immolation, but simply in the ordinary, uninteresting actuality of our own everyday life.

hen, in the deep silence, wisdom begins to sing her unending, sunlit, inexpressible song: the private song she speaks to the solitary soul. It is his own song and hers—the unique, irreplaceable song that each soul sings for himself with the unknown Spirit, as he sits on the doorstep of his own being, the place where his existence opens out into the abyss of God's nameless, limitless freedom. It is the song that each one of us must sing, the song of grace that God has composed Himself, that He may sing it within us. It is the song of His mercy for *us*, which, if we do not listen to it, will never be sung. And if we do not join with God in singing this song, we will never be fully real: for it is the song of our own life welling up like a stream out of the very heart of God's creative and redemptive love.

Each man's individual song that he sings in secret with the Spirit of God blends also in secret with the unheard notes of every other individual song. The voice of all who love God, the living and the dead, those who are on earth, those who suffer in the place of probation, those who have gone into the place of victory and rest: these voices all form a choir whose music is heard only in the depths of silence, because it is more silent than the silence itself.

I stand among you as one who offers a small message of hope, that first, there are always people who dare to seek on the margin of society, who are not dependent on social acceptance, not dependent on social routine, and prefer a kind of free-floating existence under a state of risk. And among these people, if they are faithful to their own calling, to their own vocation, and to their own message from God, communication on the deepest level is possible.

And the deepest level of communication is not communication, but communion.

It is wordless. It is beyond words, and it is beyond speech, and it is beyond concept. Not that we discover a new unity. We discover an older unity. My dear brothers and sisters, we are already one. But we imagine that we are not. And what we have to recover is our original unity. What we have to be is what we are.

I have had to accept the fact that my life is almost totally paradoxical. I have also had to learn gradually to get along without apologizing for the fact, even to myself. And perhaps this preface [to *A Thomas Merton Reader*] is an indication that I have not yet completely learned. No matter. It is in the paradox itself, the paradox which was and still is a source of insecurity, that I have come to find the greatest security. I have become convinced that the very contradictions in my life are in some ways signs of God's mercy to me: if only because someone so complicated and so prone to confusion and self-defeat could hardly survive for long without special mercy. And since this in no way depends on the approval of others, the awareness of it is a kind of liberation.

Paradoxically, I have found peace because I have always been dissatisfied. My moments of depression and despair turn out to be renewals, new beginnings. If I were once to settle down and be satisfied with the surface of life, with its divisions and its clichés, it would be time to call in the undertaker . . . . So, then, this dissatisfaction which sometimes used to worry me and has certainly, I know, worried others, has helped me in fact to move freely and even gaily with the stream of life. My unspoken (or spoken) protests have kept me from clinging to what was already done with. When a thought is done, let go of it. When something has been written, publish it, and go on to something else. You may say the same thing again someday, on a deeper level. No one needs to have a compulsion to be utterly and perfectly "original" in every word he writes. All that matters is that the old be recovered on a new plane and be, itself, a new reality. This, too, gets away from you. So let it get away.

All life tends to grow like this, in mystery inscaped with paradox and contradiction, yet centered, in its very heart, on the divine mercy. Such is my philosophy, and it is more than a philosophy—because it consists not in statements about a truth that cannot adequately be stated, but in grace, mercy, and the realization of the "new life" that is in us who believe, by the gift of the Holy Spirit. Without this gift we would have no philosophy, for we could never experience such simplicity in the midst of contradiction. Without the grace of God there could be no unity, no simplicity in our lives: only contradiction. We can overlay the contradiction with statements and explanations, we can produce an illusory coherence, we can impose on life our intellectual systems, and we can enforce upon our minds a certain strained and artificial peace. But this is not peace.

When a man enters a monastery he has to stand before the community, and formally responds to a ritual question: *Quid petis?* "What do you ask?" His answer is not that he seeks a happy life, or escape from anxiety, or freedom from sin, or moral perfection, or the summit of contemplation. The answer is that he seeks *mercy.* "The mercy of God and of the Order." Whatever else it may do, this book [*A Thomas Merton Reader*] should bear witness to the fact that I have found what I sought and continue to find it. The Order has been patient with me, God has been merciful to me, and more, countless readers have given me a gift of friendship and of love which is to me precious beyond estimation.

These readers sometimes write to me, and generally I am not able to reply. But here at least let me assure them of my gratitude, my love, and my prayers. They are in my silence, in my Mass, and in my solitude. I hope we will be together in Paradise.

7 | EPILOGUE: THE DOOR TO THE CLEAR LIGHT

Such is the door that ends all doors:

the unbuilt, the impossible, the undestroyed,

through which all the fires go

when they have "gone out."

THE ASIAN JOURNAL

The three doors (they are one door):

1. The door of emptiness. Of no-where. Of no place for a self, which cannot be entered by a self. And therefore is of no use to someone who is going somewhere. Is it a door at all? The door of no-door.

2. The door without sign, without indicator, without information. Not particularized. Hence no one can say of it "This is it! This is *the door*." It is not recognizable as a door. It is not led up to by other things pointing to it: "We are not it, but that is it—the door." No signs saying "Exit." No use looking for indications. Any door with a sign on it, any door that proclaims itself to be a door, is not the door. But do not look for a sign saying "Not-door." Or even "No Exit."

3. The door without wish. The undesired. The unplanned door. The door never expected. Never wanted. Not desirable as door. Not a joke, not a trap door. Not select. Not exclusive. Not for a few. Not for many. Not *for*. Door without aim. Door without end. Does not respond to a key—so do not imagine you have a key. Do not have your hopes on possession of the key.

There is no use asking for it. Yet you must ask. Who? For what? When you have asked for a list of all the doors, this one is not on the list. When you have asked the numbers of all the doors, this one is without a number. Do not be deceived into thinking this door is merely hard to find and difficult to open. When sought it fades. Recedes. Diminishes. Is nothing. There is no threshold. No footing. It is not empty space. It is neither this world nor another. It is not based on anything. Because it has no foundation, it is the end of sorrow. Nothing remains to be done. Therefore there is no threshold, no stop, no advance, no recessing, no entry, no non-entry. Such is the door that ends all doors: the unbuilt, the impossible, the undestroyed, through which all the fires go when they have "gone out."

Christ said, "I am the door." The nailed door. The cross, they nail the door shut with death. The resurrection: "You see, I am *not* a door." "Why do you look up to heaven?" *Attolite portas principes vestras:* "Lift up your heads, O gates." For what? The King of Glory. *Ego sum ostium:* I am the door. I am the opening, the "shewing," the revelation, the door of light, the Light itself. "I am the Light," and the light is in the world from the beginning. (It seemed to be darkness.)

SOURCES

AJ   *The Asian Journal of Thomas Merton.* New York: New Directions, 1973.

CP   *Contemplative Prayer.* Introduction by Thich Nhat Hanh. Garden City, NY: Doubleday & Company, 1969.

CWA   *Contemplation in a World of Action.* Garden City, NY: Doubleday & Company, 1971.

DQ   *Disputed Questions.* New York: Harcourt Brace Jovanovich & Company, 1960/1985.

HR   *"Honorable Reader": Reflections on My Work.*
New York: The Crossroad Publishing Company, 1991.

IE   *The Inner Experience: Notes on Contemplation.*
William H. Shannon, ed. San Francisco:
HarperSanFrancisco, 2004.

LL   *Love and Living.* Naomi Burton Stone and
Brother Patrick Hart, eds. New York: Farrar, Straus and
Giraux, 1979.

MJ   *The Monastic Journey.* Patrick Hart, ed. Garden
City, NY: Doubleday & Company, 1978.

NM   *The New Man.* New York: Farrar, Straus and
Giroux, 1961.

NMI   *No Man Is an Island*. New York, 1955.

NSC   *New Seeds of Contemplation*. New York:
New Directions, 1972.

OB   *Opening the Bible*. Collegeville, MN: Liturgical
Press, 1970.

PPE   *Peace in the Post-Christian Era*. Patricia A.
Burton, ed. Maryknoll, NY: Orbis Books, 2004.

RU   *Raids on the Unspeakable*. New York: New
Directions, 1966.

SC   *Seasons of Celebration: Meditations on the Cycle
of Liturgical Feasts*. New York: Farrar, Straus and
Giroux, 1977.

SL   *The Silent Life*. New York: Farrar, Straus and Giroux, 1996.

TMR   *A Thomas Merton Reader*. Thomas P. McDonnell, ed. NY: Doubleday & Company, 1989.

TS   *Thoughts in Solitude*. New York: Farrar, Straus and Giroux.

WD   *The Wisdom of the Desert*. New York: New Directions, 1970.

REFERENCES

page 15: TS, 78

page 17: MJ, 62

page 18: CWA, 161

page 19: CWA, 164–165

page 20: CWA, 168–169

page 21: CWA, 169

page 22: HR, 88

page 23: NMI, 16

page 24: CWA, 169–170

page 25: CWA, 170

page 26: RU, 61

page 27: CWA, 170–171

page 28: CWA, 171

page 29: AJ, 342

page 30: AJ, 342–343

page 31: CWA, 171

page 32: OB, 64

page 33: OB, 64–65

page 34: OB, 65

page 35: TMR, 18

page 36: PPE, 135

page 37: LL, 3

page 38: LL, 4

page 39: LL, 8

page 40: LL, 5

page 41: NSC, 296–297

page 42: NSC, 297

page 43: WD, 11

page 45: HR, 40–41

page 46: HR, 41

page 47: NSC, 1

page 48: NSC, 2

page 49: CWA, 174

page 50: CWA, 178–179

page 51: HR, 88

page 52: HR, 89

page 53: HR, 90

page 54: HR, 90-91

page 55: HR, 91

page 56: SC, 209–210

page 57: HR, 85-86

page 58: HR, 86

page 59: HR, 86

page 60: AJ, 117

page 61: HR, 111

page 62: HR, 113–114

page 64: HR, 135

page 65: HR, 86–87

page 66: HR, 87–88

page 67: HR, 89

page 68: HR, 64

page 69: CWA, 109–110

page 70: HR, 39

page 71: HR, 85

page 72: CWA, 353–354

page 73: CWA, 149

page 74: NSC, 3

page 75: HR, 67

page 77: HR, 91

page 79: CP, 90

page 80: CGB, 158

page 81: NM, 8–9

page 83: CP, 68–69

page 85: CP, 68

page 86: CP, 67

page 87: CP, 29–30

page 88: CP, 25

page 89: SC, 210–211

page 90: SC, 19–20

page 91: SC, 30

page 92: SC, 21

page 93: SC, 22

page 94: SC, 24

page 95: AJ, 306–307

page 96: CP, 24

page 97: CWA, 129

page 98: CP, 101

page 99: TS, 83

page 101: TS, 94

page 103: NMI, 258

page 104: NMI, 260

page 105: TS, 13

page 106: NMI, 257

page 107: TS, 91

page 108: HR, 115

page 109: DQ, 195

page 110: HR, 116

page 111: HR, 116–117

page 112: TS, 96

page 113: DQ, 183

page 114: DQ, 206–207

page 115: TS, 12

page 116: SC, 213

page 117: TS, 51

page 118: TS, 101

page 119: MJ, 198

page 120: DQ, 109

page 122: DQ, 194

page 123: TS, 118

page 124: TS, 74

page 125: SL, 3

page 126: SL, 6

page 127: TS, 56

page 129: IE, 1

page 130: IE, 29–30

page 131: IE, 33

page 132: IE, 34

page 133: IE, 35–36

page 135: IE, 36

page 136: IE, 36–37

page 137: IE, 51

page 139: IE, 53

page 140: IE, 53

page 141: IE, 54

page 142: IE, 54

page 143: IE, 54–55

page 144: IE, 55

page 145: IE, 58

page 146: IE, 59

page 147: IE, 59

page 148: IE, 59

page 149: IE, 116

page 150: IE, 117

page 151: CWA, 345

page 153: SL, vii

page 154: HR, 65

page 155: HR, 65–66

page 156: HR, 66

page 157: HR, 66

page 158: SC, 211

page 159: SC, 207–208

page 160: SC, 207

page 161: CWA, 345

page 162: AJ, 306

page 163: AJ, 307

page 164: SC, 213–214

page 165: SC, 214

page 166: SC, 214

page 167: SC, 215

page 168: AJ, 307–308

page 169: TMR, 16

page 170: TMR, 16

page 171: TMR, 17

page 172: TMR, 18

page 173: AJ, 154

page 175: AJ, 153–154

page 177: AJ, 154

page 178: AJ, 154–155

ABOUT THOMAS MERTON

Thomas Merton (1915–1968) was a writer and Trappist monk at Our Lady of Gethsemani Abbey in Kentucky. He is the author of more than seventy books that include such classics as his autobiography *The Seven Storey Mountain, New Seeds of Contemplation, Faith and Violence* and *Conjectures of a Guilty Bystander*. He is regarded as one of the most significant religious writers of the last half of the twentieth century whose work is widely appreciated as prophetic for the twenty-first.

ABOUT SOUNDS TRUE

Sounds True was founded in 1985 with a clear vision: to disseminate spiritual wisdom. Located in Boulder, Colorado, Sounds True publishes teaching programs that are designed to educate, uplift, and inspire. We work with many of the leading spiritual teachers, thinkers, healers, and visionary artists of our time.

To receive a free catalog of tools and teachings for personal and spiritual transformation, please visit www.soundstrue.com, call toll-free 800-333-9185, or write to us at the address below.

SOUNDS TRUE
PO Box 8010 / Boulder CO 80306